JAMIE VARDY'S HAVING A PARTY: LEICESTER CITY'S MIRACLE SEASON

By David Gardner

Immediate Books 2016

Published by Immediate Books, Laguna Beach, CA

http://immediatebooks.com/

First published: June 2016

Cover design by Keith Groshans

Photo courtesy Trinity Mirror plc

MMJS

*Even now there are moments when I shake my head at the madness of it all –
going from the factory floor and playing Sunday morning pub football with my
mates, to scoring for my country against the World Cup winners in Berlin. It's the
stuff of dreams. It hasn't always been an easy journey, some doubted that I was
capable, and at times I was probably guilty of not helping myself, but nobody can
question my passion for football or my commitment once I set foot on the pitch.
There is so much that people don't know and I look forward to sharing all of that
and more in what I hope will be an entertaining and inspiring story.* Jamie Vardy,
My Story, 2016

Chat s*** get banged - Jamie Vardy, Facebook, September 28, 2011

lovin life, gettin paid, and gettin laid - Jamie Vardy, Facebook, September 17,
2007

Everything I'm touching is going in. Long may that continue, Jamie Vardy, November, 2015

CONTENTS

There is something quintessentially English about Jamie Vardy that allows us to forgive his transgressions and forget the fact that this blue collar sporting hero is earning double the money in one week that most families live on for an entire year.

His rise from non-league obscurity is often compared to Roy of the Rovers but Vardy, in truth, has little in common with the teetotalling, scrupulously fair comic book captain who would never question a referee, let alone wag an angry finger in his face.

No, the reason why the great footballing public has taken Jamie Vardy to their hearts is that he is one of their own. He hasn't been cosseted and pampered like many modern day players more interested in tweeting about their cars than earning their obscenely inflated salaries.

Vardy chases lost causes, he runs until his legs give out, he scores, of course, and he appears to love every single minute he's out on the pitch.

We need to recognize ourselves in sport, even if we know that in large part it's an illusion.

It's why we can watch a man most of us had never heard of this time last year and will him to score for a team we never cared about.

The incredible story of Leicester City's miracle season under the charmingly effective Claudio Ranieri has been a joy to behold. Their Premier League triumph will undoubtedly go down as one of the greatest, if not the greatest, in the history of team sports.

We can admire the tenacity of N'Golo Kante, swoon at the silky skills of Riyad Mahrez and applaud the precise distribution of Danny Drinkwater. But Jamie Vardy remains the enduring symbol of the little engine that could.

He, more than any of the others, battled seemingly insurmountable odds just to get to the Premier League. That he conquered it was as much a surprise to him as it was to us.

No wonder Leicester's fans have been singing all year that he's having a party.

His story offers hope to every Sunday league player turning out in the cow field behind the pub; for every disillusioned youngster battling to be noticed by the mercenary-funded top tier teams who prefer to look abroad than in their own back yards; for every worker everywhere who pins their hopes on hard work and commitment ahead of position and privilege.

The Sheffield-born striker kept going through the muddy backwaters of English football, where crowds of a couple of hundred constitute a big gate and a portaloo might double as a changing room. Why wouldn't he play his heart out on the stately grounds of the Premier League?

With his 24 goals and 6 assists for Leicester, and another two strikes for England, Vardy proved all the doubters wrong in a single season.

There is a darker side to Vardy's personality, one perhaps more in step with many young men rousting about on a Saturday night than we would care to think about. His drinking habits got him into hot water with the law and his more recent boorish behaviour, caught on camera at a casino, calling a fellow gambler a "Jap" was unacceptable.

He should be called to account for these indiscretions, especially now that impressionable young fans follow his every move. But his popularity in a melting pot Leicester City dressing room tends to suggest something rather different.

On the Monday night when Leicester City's season was hanging in the balance, when Tottenham Hotspur still had an opportunity to crash the party, most of the 1st team headed to Vardy's house to watch the game together.

Some confessed they were ready to go home at half-time when home team Chelsea fell two behind and looked unlikely to fight back for the draw that would guarantee Leicester the Premier League trophy.

But the hundreds of fans that gathered outside Vardy's Leicestershire mansion wouldn't have approved.

The video footage published the next morning by defender Robert Fuchs showed just what a party at the Vardy's could be; wild scenes of celebration from players who really wanted to believe all season long and now they truly could; Leicester City were the champions of England.

Jamie Party's having a party.

Yes indeed.

The striker with the scruffy mohawk had just scored his second for non-league Stocksbridge Park Steels in the eighth tier of English football and looked likely to hit a hatful more in the key away game when the call came from the touchline.

"Vardy, it's time." The call boomed out from the touchline, partially lost in the clatter of pelting rain on the solitary metal-roof terrace.

Jamie Vardy, then 23-years-old, raced off the pitch showing the blistering pace he'd tantalized defenders with all that muddy Saturday afternoon in 2007. He didn't stop to talk to the coach but grabbed his kit bag from the makeshift changing room at Belper Town's home ground in Derbyshire and ran for the fence, leaping through a gap in the rusty railings.

"I kept him on probably a bit longer than I should," recalled former Stocksbridge manager Gary Morrow. "His mum appeared, he came straight off, jumped over the fence and ran off in his kit and boots and everything."

Outside the ground, his crane worker dad, Phil, was sitting waiting in his car looking anxiously at his watch. The time was 4.15pm. He had been waiting for 15 minutes.

Throwing his dirty bag in the back seat, Vardy, still wearing his muddy boots, jumped in the passenger seat. "Okay, let's go...sorry I'm late."

"You were coming off after 60 minutes." Phil Vardy was worried about the Saturday afternoon traffic on the M1 back to Sheffield. "We have to be back by 6pm. You know that. The traffic's a mess."

"Yeah but I got another goal. I thought I could snatch a quick third."

It was always the same at away games, cutting it so fine Vardy often had to sprint from the car into the family home with literally seconds to spare.

Father and son barely spoke during the journey south. His wife Lisa was biting her nails, looking down at her watch every few minutes. The M1 was gridlocked.

"We'll make it fine, dad, don't worry." Vardy pulled down his sock and scratched at the electronic bracelet around his ankle. "Just one more month and we won't have to do this any more."

With that, Phil turned the corner and pulled up outside the house. "Go! Jamie, go!"

Vardy threw open the car door and hurtled the 50ft to the front door, turning with a triumphant smile the moment he reached the front step. It was 5.57 pm.

"Made it!"

Vardy was five months through a six months home detention sentence for criminal assault. He had to be home between the hours of 6 pm and 6 am seven days a week, or face a possible prison term. The tag around his ankle ensured the authorities knew if he broke the curfew, even by a few minutes.

"If the away games were too far, I could only play an hour and they'd have to take me off," Vardy said later.

"It was a case of hope we were winning, jump over the fence and straight in my parents' car to make sure I was home in time. That was for six months.

"You could wear the tag like an ankle guard. There was no way of breaking it, even if you got kicked. You could hit it with a hammer and it's not coming off!"

10

As countless defenders over the years can attest, "Vards" may be skinny but he's tough. He came from Hillsborough, a working class suburb of Sheffield where the locals had a reputation for being as hard as steel.

After Vardy got drawn into a pub brawl not far from his home, he insisted he didn't start the trouble. But friends said his two attackers quickly regretted crossing him.

"I'd been out with a friend who wore a hearing aid and two lads thought it would be funny to start mocking him," he explained.

"They got thrown out of the pub but they were waiting for us an hour and half later. They started attacking him and I wasn't going to stand there and let him take a beating.

"I'm not proud of what I did but I defended him, which I'd always do for a mate, and it got me in trouble. That's one of the things that's made me the person I am. It was hard. It has an effect on your family. All my mates were out enjoying themselves and I was locked in the house. Luckily I had a big DVD collection.

"It was something I had to learn from and I did."

As far as Jamie Vardy has come since then, he never shies away from discussing his hardscrabble past. It is essential to his make-up, an indelible component to his sensational rise from non-league journeyman player to the most feared and deadly striker in the biggest football league in the world.

These days, he drives to work in a £168,000 Bentley, he lives in a £1 million mansion in Melton Mowbray - scene of the infamous party held the night Tottenham Hotspurs drew to confirm Leicester's EPL triumph - and earns £80,000-a-week.

"Vards" has come a long way since racing home from away games to avoid a bleak spell behind bars. But then, so has every member of the Leicester City dream team that proved everyone wrong and became the greatest underdog champions in the history of sport.

Here's the untold story of how a team of cast-offs, journeymen and also-rans went from bottom of the league relegations survivors and 5,000-to-1 no-hopers to champions of the English Premier League in the space of just 12 months.

Yes, Jamie Vardy's having a party. But the striker and his teammates are not alone. Bookmaker William Hill had to pay out £3 million to punters who believed the impossible could happen - and the entire football world is still celebrating a sporting miracle that may never be matched.

The Leicester City players had been focusing on playing one game at a time and tuning out all the expectations for so many weeks that their emotions at the final whistle were more about incredulity than joy.

The excited faces in the crowd at the King Power Stadium were much the same, some streaked with blue and white paint that had merged in the afternoon downpour, all wreathed in smiles of astonishment.

The script had run to perfection right to the end with Jamie Vardy, the team's goalscoring talisman, netting two, and Andy King, the club's most loyal servant, claiming the other in a mismatched final home game against Everton on May 5, 2016.

Goalkeeper Kasper Schmeichal stalked his penalty area with a sour face after giving up a goal to ruin his clean sheet but he couldn't hold onto it for long. The result didn't really matter. The team, the city and most of Britain were just waiting for the final whistle.

The result coming through several days earlier from Stamford Bridge, when Chelsea fought tooth and nail for a 2-2 draw that ended Spurs' final surge, had launched the celebrations.

Long-serving midfielder Andy King was among the first team players to gather at Vardy's home hoping for the best the previous Monday evening.

"We arrived totally buzzing, thinking, 'Could this be the night that it happens?" he told the Daily Mail. "Then at half-time, it was like, 'You got any water, Vards? We have training tomorrow'.' It was gonna be, 'See you in the morning'.

'Nobody actually left at half-time but I think we might have. We stayed because there were people outside and it would have looked so bad being photographed going in and then sneaking away at half-time.

'After the (Gary) Cahill goal we knew Chelsea would get another chance. It got nasty after that. Chelsea were in their faces and Tottenham lost their cool, understandably. Then (Eden) Hazard. What a goal. The place just went mad.'

"It was pretty wild towards the end," recalled Vardy's wife, Becky. "Some of the lads started to leave at around 4:30am.

"It was a special night. I was running around hosting all these crazy boys, getting them drinks, making food and just watching the moment unfold. Amazingly our daughter Sofia was asleep upstairs the whole time! Her bedroom is above the kitchen, she's 18 months old but she didn't even move!"

Vardy later revealed things got so out of hand the players broke his TV. Some millionaire players might have bought a new one; he got it fixed.

But the celebrations were only just beginning. Solid pros that they are, the Leicester players were back in training the next day nursing their sore heads.

Back at the KP, the clock running down with Leicester ahead by a comfortable margin in their final home game of the season, referee Anthony Taylor's whistle caused pandemonium.

Captain Wesley Morgan bumped heads with the redoubtable Polish stand-in centre back Marcin Wasilewski and the players in blue fell into one another's arms across the pitch as those in white quietly slipped down the tunnel towards a summer full of mid-table recriminations.

Given a guarantee of Everton's mid-table finish at the start of the season, Leicester would almost certainly have taken it.

14

But that was before. This was now. And Leicester had turned every expectation on its head.

Manchester City was left fending off Manchester United for a place in the Champions League; Tottenham was still trying (and failing) to finish above arch foes Arsenal for the first time in forever. But Leicester were the champions of England - and they had already secured their place in the following year's Champion's League, the zenith of world club football.

Richard Scudamore, Premier League executive chairman, hailed Leicester's success as historic and admitted it has "made mugs of us all."

He added: "Nobody saw it coming and even when it was halfway through the season nobody said it could be sustained.

'It's probably the biggest sporting story ever and the biggest sporting achievement ever. In terms of an overall story, as an overall achievement, it is absolutely the best."

The Premier League suits had all week to choreograph the trophy ceremony and they didn't disappoint. The crowds had been gathering outside the King Power for five hours before kick-off, and a giant screen was set up for those unable to snag a ticket. It was like a Super Bowl tailgate party except pretty much everyone was supporting the same side.

Rain had turned to tears before the game as Andrea Bocelli sang 'Nessun Dorma' and 'Time to Say Goodbye,' with his friend Claudio Ranieri lachrymose alongside on a dais stacked with flowers.

The small matter of a game of football delayed the festivities for the 90 minutes that followed. Then the celebrations proper could really begin.

From Club Ambassador Alan Birchenall bringing out the trophy with a smile on his face as wide as the Castle Yard, to Captain Morgan and Ranieri

15

taking a jug handle each to lift it to the skies, the King Power was rocking on its foundations.

Even the bizarre procession of Leicester City's Thai owner and chairman Vichai Srivaddhanaprabha parading around the field with one of his entourage carrying a Thai royal portrait seemed to fit perfectly into the surreal occasion.

"Pinch me," said one lifelong fan to his son. "I'm going to wake up any moment and find out we're back in League One."

But he would have awoken to the Sunday morning papers emblazoned in Leicester City blue and the knowledge that he truly had witnessed a bona fide miracle.

"They did it," said Sky commentator Martin Tyler. "The greatest story ever told..."

The most important day in Claudio Ranieri's life was as delightfully idiosyncratic as his first season with Leicester City.

While his entire team assembled at Jamie Vardy's house to watch Chelsea and Spurs bludgeon one another into the draw that confirmed the Foxes as champions, Ranieri flew to Rome for lunch with his 96-year-old mother, Renata.

Most people teetering on the brink of history may have felt justified in breaking a date with their mum, but the veteran Italian manager isn't most people.

It's funny how winning changes perspectives. Had his team been fighting relegation, Ranieri's European break would have perhaps been viewed as a dereliction of duty. As it turned out, the media was more interested in what he was eating than how he was coping. This was Italy, after all.

"We had some steak with chicory. Before leaving, he ate strawberries with lemon and sugar," Renata told the Italian newspaper La Repubblica.

"My son has to keep himself in shape, so he rarely asks for a starter. He talked about Leicester a bit, but wanted to relax. He was with me for two hours, then said the president of his team had organised a plane to take him back to England. We said goodbye and he went towards the Ciampino airport."

She added: "At the final whistle I burst into tears. I only heard from Claudio later because first my grandchildren and my son's cousins called. He was so happy. We all are. Now we can finally relax.

"I watched every game, it was a continual series of emotions. He calls me every evening and kept me up to date on everything. This morning I bought the sports papers and saw the headlines. It was satisfying.

"I have to admit, I did not expect him to win with Leicester. He found these players … they are good lads. He told me they always trained as real professionals.

"Naturally it wasn't a big squad full of champions. I know that he's happy in England, they always treated him perfectly. He rediscovered himself there."

Unlike his team, Ranieri boasted a prestigious resume of big clubs; Chelsea, Inter Milan, Juventus and Roma among them. But through 30 years of management across four of Europe's top leagues - Spain, England, Italy and France - he was always the nearly man; always the bridesmaid.

His zenith in the various leagues had been second place finishes with Chelsea, Juventus, Roma and Monaco. The critics complained he didn't have the ruthless streak to close out a successful campaign, that he lacked the ferocity of a Jose Mourinho or Sir Alex Ferguson.

When he arrived back in England after an 11-year absence to take over the reins of lowly Leicester, there were some serious questions about his credentials in spite of his popularity among the media.

His teams had always pulled up just short and the 64-year-old Roman had just been sacked as the Greek national team coach after a humiliating home loss to the Faroe Islands. Even Gary Lineker, Match of the Day pundit and one of the Foxes favourite sons, tweeted at the time: "Claudio Ranieri? Really?"

Despite being nicknamed the "Tinkerman" during his four seasons at Chelsea due to his habit of changing the line-up, Ranieri relied on a small squad at Leicester, leaving the core of the team and a simple 4-4-2 system virtually unchanged.

Jamie Vardy insists he wasn't worried about the Italian's arrival at the KP, despite being given his chance at Leicester by the outgoing Pearson. "I wasn't worried. He's helping me and the team out defensively He's let me be more free."

Sometimes his methods could be unorthodox, even slightly bizarre.

When he felt his defence was giving away too many goals, Ranieri came up with a very Italian solution, promising a pizza party if they could keep a clean sheet. A 1-0 win at Crystal Palace in October stopped the rot - and earned the players their pizzas. For the rest of the season, the Leicester defence remained one of the tightest in the league as the team ground out low-scoring victories.

Keeping expectations low, claiming even when his team topped the division that he was focusing on avoiding relegation, Ranieri expertly shouldered the growing pressure by playing down Leicester's chances.

"Dilly-ding, dilly-dong," he finally exclaimed when his team's Champions League qualification was no longer in any doubt, making public a catchphrase that had already caught on with his players during training.

It all sounded very naive and simple when it was anything but. When everyone in football was waiting for his team to crack, Ranieri was happy to make cracks and act the innocent when he knew very well that the only people his players had to fear were themselves. As long as they kept believing, they could make it happen. If the doubt started to creep in, that would be the beginning of the end.

Claudio Ranieri doesn't fit the image of the larger than life football manager. He is a collector of art, a lover of antiques and literature, a cultured man. His image couldn't have been any different to the man he was replacing, Nigel Pearson, who liked to hide his love for the game behind a hard-nosed pragmatism.

Ranieri was 48 when he arrived in London to take over from Giunluca Vialli at Stamford Bridge and hardly spoke a word of English. The son of a butcher, he enjoyed London's restaurants - particularly Lebanese and Indian - eschewing the culinary snobbery of less knowledgeable foreign visitors.

His days away from the team were spent perusing antique fairs with his wife, Dr. Rosanna Ranieri, an art teacher who ran a shop called 'Retro in Rome' selling designer ware from the Sixties in their native Rome.

"When we are together in London we go looking for furniture, glass and porcelain," he said in 2002, adding "at the moment we are looking for furniture from the Fifties, the minimalist style."

Ranieri was happy to talk about football, but other things, too. He was as adroit discussing Monet, Van Gogh and Picasso as he was Ronaldo, Rossi or Zidane.

It was perhaps forgotten that when he arrived in Leicester he made his name as a manager not by shepherding highly priced world stars, but in getting the very best out of modest squads with teams like Cagliari.

Asked what books he was reading for a story in the London Evening Standard, Ranieri answered: "I do not have much time for relaxation but when I can, I like to read. The books are in Italian because by the time I come home late at the end of the day, I am very tired and it is difficult to learn English.

20

"The first book I am reading is by an Italian journalist named Beppe Severgnini. The title is Inglesi and it is all about the English, what makes them tick. The second book is Leadership, by the former Mayor of New York Rudolph Giuliani, and the third book chronicles the life of a priest who had a church in Naples and worked with street children."

"Three? So, you even rotate your books?" the Standard's football reporter Ken Dyer joked to the Tinker Man.

A moment of silence was followed by two minutes of uncontrollably joyous laughter from Ranieri, who finally composed himself to add: "Yes, rotating the books. You tell them Claudio even rotates the books."

Born in Rome in 1951, he won nine trophies in his career, but never a top-flight league title before this year. Previously, his biggest successes were the Coppa Italia in 1996 and the Copa Del Rey in 1999.

Ranieri spent 18 months at his hometown club, Roma, but resigned in February 2011 after falling out with club officials. Renata believes success in England has allowed her son to finally put that disappointment behind him.

"In my view, at Roma he was not treated with respect. In the family we are all Giallorossi fans, so when Claudio was there we were also guests at Trigoria [the training ground]," she said. "We were disappointed with the way things ended. Look, he won his own *scudetto* here too, because he went really close, but he arrived after the season had already started. Now he's 'King of England', imagine that."

"I told them, if you keep a clean sheet, I'll buy pizza for everybody. I think they're waiting for me to offer a hot dog too."

"From the beginning when something was wrong I've been saying: 'Dilly-ding, dilly-dong, wake up, wake up!' So on Christmas Day I bought for all the players and all the staff a little bell."

"Why can't we continue to run, run, run? We are like Forrest Gump. Leicester is Forrest Gump."

Sitting next to one another on the bench at Sheffield Wednesday as young teenagers, Liam Muirhead and Jamie Vardy could never have guessed where their football lives would take them more than a decade-and-a-half later.

For Vardy, his long and often gruelling rollercoaster rise through the leagues would culminate in an incredible 2016 season as one of the EPL's top scoring strikers with champions Leicester City and a starting place in the team representing England at Euro 2016.

Liam's similarly circuitous soccer journey took him through a series of professional clubs and across the Atlantic to California. There he is busy passing on the knowledge he gained playing alongside some of the best in the game to lucky youngsters at Spartans FC in Yucaipa where he is Director of Coaching.

"I was with Vardy from the age of 9 to 15 at Sheffield Wednesday and I left for Leeds United about 6 months before he was let go. We sat on the bench together," recalled Liam. "Me and Jamie Vardy were the smallest on the team at the time. We didn't get to play a lot. We were very skinny and we were released. But we were still growing - now I'm 6ft 2 ins and Vardy's about 6ft 1 ins.

"I always remember playing Liverpool at the Academy and the coaches called us and told us we would be playing the younger team, which kind of devastated us because they thought we weren't good enough."

Liam moved on to play in the Leeds United youth team with Danny Rose, who went on to star for Spurs, and James Milner, who went from Manchester City to Liverpool - both current England players - as well as Aaron Lennon (Everton) and ex-international goalkeeper Scott Carson (Derby County) before heading across the Atlantic.

Vardy didn't move so far away, but his football trajectory eventually started moving in an altogether different direction - upwards.

"I only really started taking note when he scored in the championship and I thought, *Oh! Jamie Vardy, how did he get there?*"

One thing is for certain; he didn't take the easy route.

Jamie Richard Vardy was born on January 11, 1987, the son of labourer Richard Gill and Lisa Clewes, an assistant in a Sheffield solicitor's office.

Gill met Lisa, who was six years his junior, at the Old Crown pub on London Road, Sheffield, and they quickly became a couple despite the qualms of her parents who worried about the age difference.

When Lisa fell pregnant, Gill moved into her parent's home and for a while, at least, they tried to care for the baby together.

"It didn't go well," Gill told the Mail on Sunday. "I used to feed him and change him and push him out in the pram – but her parents did not approve of me."

Within months, Gill began an affair and got another woman pregnant. "I behaved badly," he told the Mail. "It is a real shame that things did not turn out differently. But his mother and I were really young and I completely lost touch with them."

When Gill said he lost touch he wasn't joking. He didn't realise Vardy was his son until midway through Leicester's triumphant 2015/16 season.

"'I am completely overwhelmed and staggered to find out how famous my son is," he confessed. "Until last week, I had never even heard of Jamie Vardy, let alone realised that he was my son.

"I am not really interested in football. But now I will be watching the results more closely and following his career. If he would like to meet me, that

24

would be great but I understand he might not want to have anything to do with me. Either way, it's been fantastic watching him play. I will remember that for the rest of my life."

It wasn't too long before Lisa married the man Vardy would call "dad" - crane operator Phillip Vardy - and the family settled into a working class terraced home in the inner city shadows of Sheffield Wednesday's Hillsborough stadium.

In school, he had just one thought on his mind; to become a professional footballer and, for a while at least, he appeared to have all the potential to make his dreams come true, signing as a schoolboy apprentice for Sheffield Wednesday at the age of eight and playing in the Championship club's academy.

But his world fell apart after he was released at 15 and his family worried he'd go off the rails.

"I had a growth spurt - suddenly shot up 20 centimetres - literally a month after I got released. That made it even worse," he recalled.

Unable to sign for another professional team, the despondent teen quit football altogether and started a sports science course at a technology college in nearby Rotherham.

With the focus of football gone, Vardy struggled to get back on track, but it wasn't easy to fill the void. At the Thomas Rotherham College he developed a reputation as a prankster.

One of his teachers, Chris Wall, told BBC Radio: "He was funny, he was a bit mischievous - a lovable rogue. When he was with the footballers in the changing rooms he used to hide other players kit. Boots would go missing - he'd hide them in the false ceiling in the changing room."

If his college teammates were irritated they quickly forgave him. Even then he was such a selfless team player that he could virtually do no wrong.

As the world now knows, Vardy's best position is centre forward. But he never complained when his college coach played him in defence.

"He loved a challenge," recalled Chris Wall. "He always got stuck in well. He was quick, he had a great engine, he could run all day. He actually played wingback rather than centre forward for us. He was so quick and he challenged and he covered such an immense amount of ground."

But it wasn't a good time. Vardy got in with a bad crowd and, without the discipline of regular training, there was no longer any need to worry about the hours he kept or the amount he was drinking.

He had no great interest in college; all he really wanted to do was play football.

Quitting his sports science course, Vardy returned to Sheffield and worked in a factory making medical prosthetics; the heavy lifting took such a toll on his back he eventually had to quit or risk permanent damage.

"I was a carbon fibre technician," he explained. "My job involved making splints for disabled people with drop-foot. We had to do a lot of lifting into hot ovens. We were continually lifting things hundreds of times a day and it was damaging my back."

This was no labour of love. Vardy was living for the weekends, for the Saturday night on the town, for the crack. There was always the Sunday morning game for the local pub to work off the hangover and perhaps the odd bruise from when things got out of hand the previous night.

The factory work wasn't causing him to miss his football. "If anything, I'd ring work some mornings and tell them I'd got injured playing, so I didn't have to work."

His sojourn from the game lasted nearly nine months before the lure of a return to football with Sheffield's Wickersley Youth team in 2003 brought a little swagger back into his life.

He may have been back at the bottom of the ladder but at least he was doing what he loved.

The break had reignited Vardy's enjoyment for the game that had steadily been eroded in all the years he spent on the sidelines at Wednesday.

"Jamie became very disenchanted with football," Len Curtis, chairman of Wickersley, said in an interview. "It's like a lot of kids released from academies. They are living the dream and don't know what to do until suddenly it's taken away from them."

Curtis, a former Leeds United player, explained: "We really look after the players. We don't like aggressive managers; we like those who bring the players on. That's the type of club Jamie came into."

At the time, says Curtis, Vardy "was lost to football. He didn't know what to do, where to go. He had five months out of the game, and he put on weight.

"The sheer raw nature of junior football—playing on grass pitches that aren't the best, parents of other opposition screaming at you, rough kids in Sheffield—he grew up into a man at Wickersley."

After being released by Sheffield Wednesday, Vardy "felt rejected," Curtis said. "He hadn't had much love, and we just put an arm around him. He would have come to us quite troubled. He didn't quite know where to go, but the bonding and teamwork made him part of something.

"His personality came out more. He was always quiet and shy, but his personality was always steely and confident - not afraid of playing against any-one. He's still a down-to-earth Sheffield lad. He's got no airs or graces. He knows where he's come from."

Eventually, an impressive display against Stocksbridge Park Steels brought an offer to join the bigger local club seven miles away from Sheffield, borne from the foundations of the works teams of a local British Steel plant.

The pay would ensure he didn't get carried away - £30-a-week.

Bracken Moor sits atop a steep hill in the picturesque Yorkshire coun-tryside that's more Last of the Summer Wine than the harsh environment of the Evo Stick Premier League. It was there that Vardy began his long road back to redemption in football.

A few miles outside Sheffield the fans are no less passionate than the Wednesday and United supporters about their Stocksbridge Park Steels team - and their favourite son. If there was ever any doubt that Vardy once played here it's quickly dispelled by the 450-seat Jamie Vardy Stand.

Not long released from the team he'd supported his whole life, Vardy found a supportive footballing family offering him the foundation on which he's built ever since.

Sheffield Star reporter Paul Webster remembers watching Vardy's 2002 debut for Stocksbridge.

"As soon as you saw him, you thought, Jesus Christ, he's good," he told the Yorkshire Post. "He was a bit of a scraggy kid, you looked at him and thought there was nothing to him, but he had no fear. He was up against some big centre backs that day, and he got the ball to his feet and took them on.

"I told the manager after the game that I was impressed with him.

"He had that technical ability that lots of non-league lads don't have. The first touch in particular.

"A lot of players have pace, and that's okay. What he had was that his first touch was absolutely brilliant, and you can't teach that, it's a skill. It's like a pianist. It's that natural ability he has. They would ping the ball to him from 40 or 50 yards and he would take it down on his chest. He would kill it with his first touch. It was down and under control with his foot. Then he would be past the defender."

His old Stocksbridge manager Gary Marrow decided to throw him into the first team, despite his wiry frame.

"He's obviously had a knock to his confidence being released by Sheffield Wednesday and a desire to prove people wrong," said Marrow. "We gave him that opportunity and he grabbed it with both hands."

"He is quite an aggressive footballer, and that's not common in a strik-er," said Marrow.
"He would go into tackles when he should not be tackling people. He was going into tackles that were 60/40 in the other guy's favour.

"I used to turn away at times thinking that he would break his leg. It was little things like that.

"I can remember him getting 'done' himself at Kidsgrove in his first season. It was then that we said that there was no need to go into them: 'You're going into a tackle where you will come away with the ball anyway, just stand up'."

"He kept himself to himself," said Rob Poulter, who knew Vardy at Sheffield Wednesday and played with him at Stocksbridge. "He was a young lad coming into a first team at Stocksbridge.

"Initially, he was quite quiet, got his head down and played for the team and did what was asked of him. It was when he started playing that the players realised how good he was and could be. That was when he came out of his shell.

"He's always been quiet, but when he's needed to be—like he is at the minute—he is quite vocal and in your face, but in a good way."

It wasn't long before a plethora of goals and his solid work ethic had him knocking on the door of the first team, but it wasn't so easy for him to shake his 'Jack the lad' reputation.

"As a player he was dynamic but a bit wayward," Stocksbridge chairman Allen Bethel said in an interview. "As a young boy, after he left Wednesday, he went a bit haywire with a few of his mates but from playing point of view with us, he was always first to training and last out.

"He was a terrifically fast player over five to 10 yards, he had a lot of energy although he was slight. He broke into the first team but then fell out with the manager. He immediately went into the first team on my recommendation. He was lucky.

"He played two years with [Stocksbridge manager] Gary Marrow then a lot of people started to watch him. He went to Crewe, but Dario Gradi wasn't in charge, and the manager was building an experienced side who he wanted to survive relegation, hence why he came back to us.

"We had some trouble with him, not trouble for me but trouble in the sense he was a bit of a boy, who got into trouble going into Sheffield on Saturday nights.

"[He was] a Jack the Lad but never rude to us. He did a few silly things on Saturday nights, a few people targeted him. Sheffield Wednesday came in for him, we offered them first choice as they were only six miles down the road and they said they weren't interested."

Bethel remembered the then 18-year-old Vardy torturing opposing defenders in a cup final. "Jamie had run them absolutely ragged in the first half and I was just popping over the ground for a cuppa when I heard their half-time team talk," said Bethel. "They were men 10 years and more his senior and they finished it by saying, 'kick him, stop him, just kill the b******!'"

In the second half, Vardy was kicked "up hill and down dale. He got a terrible hiding from them but not once in that 45 minutes did he kick out, complain or look over at the bench to be substituted.

"Most 18-year-olds would have been cowed by that, especially one as slight as him, but he just got his head down and ran them ragged. We won comfortably. You could tell right then that he had something special about him.

"Sheffield United came [to watch him] eight times. Neil Warnock said he'd sent one guy several times and said the club couldn't risk him because he has been sent off twice in eight games he'd been to watch. Rotherham offered £2,000 and we refused, that was Mark Robins."

Vardy's disciplinary record was putting off potential suitors - he was sent off four times in his last season at Stocksbridge.

"Playing in non-league toughened me up," Vardy recalled in an interview with the Sheffield Telegraph. "I was getting kicked and abused mercilessly by old school central defenders, and bad tackles down in those leagues might not even get a yellow card.

"There's definitely no video evidence or retrospective panels at that level! We used to have to get up way too early and then jump on a coach for four-hour drives. Then after the game you'd get an envelope with £30 in it just for playing. I was working in factories at the time. But all those experiences straightened me out."

That didn't mean he didn't still like to play pranks - and they could still get him into hot water.

It was just a few weeks after his electronic ankle tag was removed, (after his six-month night curfew for assault was completed) when Vardy got on the coach for Stocksbridge's annual end-of-season outing to Blackpool.

As usual, Vary was looking for ways to spice up the fun.

"We used to have a trip away to Blackpool and Jamie hopped into this joke shop and came out with this full rubber mask that looked quite gruesome," remembered Gary Marrow. "He put it on and then jumped out at two women PCs who virtually cleared the promenade.

"And at the time he'd only just had his tag taken off."

With the question marks over his character overriding his goalscoring prowess,
Vardy would have to wait for the big time to come calling. In the meantime, he had to settle for FC Halifax Town of the Northern Premier League who paid £16,000 for Vardy in 2010.

Again, it wasn't long before Vardy started attracting attention on the pitch. Now playing as a fully-fledged centre forward after spells on both wings earlier in his fledgling career, the recent reject was rapidly becoming one of the most talked about players in the league's lower echelons.

It didn't help that he turned up for his first day at Halifax without proper training boots, but he soon won over his teammates and his manager Neil Aspin.

Towards the end of the season he came close to scoring a hat-trick of hat-tricks but failed to find a third goal in Halifax's 3–1 win over Nantwich Town.

"The first time I've seen him he was playing in a pre-season game for Stocksbridge against Sheffield United Under-21s and I only had to watch him the one time," said Aspin. "I said to my chairman that I've seen this player and we should try and buy him."

But Aspin, a former Leeds United defender, was bemused when he turned up at Bracken Moor several times to scout Vardy only to learn that he wasn't on the team sheet. Finally, he discovered the games kicked off after Vardy's court-imposed curfew so he couldn't play.

"It's true," smiled Aspin. "Midweek games were better for me because we weren't playing and I could get away, but each time Vardy was conspicuous by his absence. I was puzzled. I couldn't understand it.

"Further discreet inquiries revealed why and I eventually caught up with Jamie in pre-season. I stood behind the goal and watched him attacking it.

"His pace was electric – that's the first thing I noticed and the clincher for me. It was his quickness that won a penalty. He had no right to reach the ball but he did, took a touch, and the defender had him over.

"What I also liked about him was his work rate and the fact that, despite playing wide, not through the middle, he would leave his foot in which is unusual for a winger.

"Vardy had been sent off three times the previous season for that but I wasn't put off. The exact opposite as it happened. I liked a player with a bit of bottle, a bit of fire in his belly. Remember, I was a centre-half noted for mixing it!

"Throughout most of that season, we were haggling over the price. We finally signed him in pre-season. We took the plunge.

"You could tell immediately that he has great potential but when he first turned up for pre-season training, he didn't have the correct footwear. All the other players who didn't know who he was looked at him and said: 'Who is that we've signed?' But once he started playing, everyone realised we had someone who was going to be a bit special.

"I was convinced within one game. He played on the right wing; he played on the left wing all in the same game. He played different positions; there was his pace, his touch, so I didn't need to see much more. I saw enough in that spell to convince us to sign him.

"I did my homework, as I do with all players I sign and I had heard reports of various of off-the-field incidents. He arrived with his manager, he didn't have an agent, he wasn't bothered about the money, it was just the chance that there would be better opportunities at Halifax.

35

"At first he was quite quiet but once he got in the dressing room and started mixing with the players, he was a bit of a live wire. If you have a lad who is willing to chase lost causes and work exceptionally hard then you settle in to the group quite easily and everyone took to him. As a manager, he never gave me any problems.

"He was playing in the league we were in and obviously he was better than the other players, and we got questions from other clubs and people were ringing me up and asking 'where do you think he can play?'

"At the time I said I thought he could play in the Championship and the reaction was, 'Well you're only trying to boost him up because you're trying to sell him'."

After one season at the Shay, during which he helped the team with promotion with a tally of 29 goals in 41 games, Vardy was on his way again, with Halifax pocketing a £134,000 profit.

Dave Riche, a former Sports Editor with the Nuneaton Evening News and now a Football Business Development Manager, witnessed the moment that really changed Vardy's fortunes and set him on the path to glory.

"On Tuesday August 23rd 2011 I was sat in Fleetwood Town chairman Andy Pilley's Jeep driving back from a humiliating 4-0 defeat away at Barrow and there was only one thing on his mind . . . Jamie Vardy," he remembered.

"Fleetwood were favourites for promotion and the chairman was determined to take his club into the Football League. He had already assembled a strike force full of experience and pace, but he wanted the final piece of his jigsaw.

"At the time Vardy was making waves with Halifax Town at the top of Conference North and a run of 27 goals in 37 games had teams looking at him, but an asking price of £150,000 plus sell-ons was required.

"In the Non League Paper – the weekly "bible" for football chairmen, managers and players, an article was written which was promoting the talents of Vardy but it was clear that a cloak and dagger approach would be needed to get his signature, with Football League clubs also in the hunt.

"As we drove back from Cumbria in horrendous conditions, the discussion in the car was about one person and the chairman was determined to get his man.

"Phone calls were made, and bartering was attempted but Halifax chairman David Bosomworth who had signed Vardy for £15,000 from Stocksbridge Park Steels just a year earlier, was determined to cash in on his investment.

"Fast forward 48 hours and a deal had been done and in the Friday night game at Highbury, the 24-year-old made his debut in a goalless draw with York City."

Vardy signed for Conference team Fleetwood Town for £150,000, with eyebrows raised over whether the skinny upstart was worth the money. It wouldn't take him very long to show how much of a bargain he was.

With a high non-league price tag around his neck, Jamie Vardy was initially looked at with suspicion by his new teammates at Fleetwood, a familiar pattern for the striker.

But it didn't take long for the joker - tagged "Steptoe" by some of his old mates - to win them over, just as he had done in all his previous dressing rooms.

Vardy was soon up to his old tricks. "I got the chef's car on his birthday," he admitted. "I wrapped his car in cling film with all the food from the day before in it... he wasn't too impressed. But his missus planned it all so it wasn't too bad.

"I do like to have a little joke in the dressing rooms."

His former 'Cod Army' teammate Rob Atkinson shared a house with Vardy for the season and he told The Sun: "Jamie was always life and soul of the parties. He liked to be at the centre of things, whether it was out with the lads having a few beers or playing pranks on his team-mates.

"In fact, even a year after he left Fleetwood he came on my stag do in Magaluf. Jamie is one of the funniest men I've met and I doubt he has changed much as a personality."

Atkinson, who went on to play for National League side Guiseley, recalled: "Hardly a day passed without something happening. He used to dress people's cars in shower gel and shaving foam or put cones on the top of them.

"He was always doing things like that — stirring things up to get a reaction from the lads.

"It was harmless fun but he got the lads laughing, which was fantastic for team spirit — and don't forget he scored 34 goals that season. He won us the league pretty much on his own. He was scoring hat-tricks and braces — all similar to the goals he scores today using his pace. Jamie could catch pigeons, he was so fast!

"Football needs characters like him. Let's face it, when you see Premier League players interviewed nowadays, it's like they're reading off a script.

"Jamie is not like that. He's such a fun, down-to-earth bloke as well as being a seriously good footballer and it's no coincidence Leicester's success has been built on a great team spirit.

"There seems to be a sense of fun and freedom about them, which is so refreshing."

Vardy drove his second-hand Saab to and from home in Sheffield to Fleetwood and would usually give Atkinson a lift in the car littered with Lucozade bottles.

"Jamie did most of the driving. He was helping me out because I had an ankle injury. He drove an old Saab 9-3. It had water and Lucozade bottles all over the back seats. He always had an energy drink in his hand," said Atkinson.

"We'd chat about our games and I tried to sniff out who was interested in him because loads of Championship clubs were after him."

The two friends lived in a four-bed Victorian terraced house before moving to a detached pad, sharing with Fleetwood team-mates Peter Till and Junior Brown.

"Jamie wasn't too clever at doing chores. I didn't ever see him get out the vacuum or ironing board — but we were four young lads living on our own!

We did all do our fair share of cleaning and drying the pots and pans. So I've no complaints about Jamie on that score," added Atkinson.

Vardy relaxed at home playing snooker, pool or darts…but he still liked to win.

"Jamie must have good hand-eye co-ordination because he was really good with the cue and chucking arrows. He wanted to win a game of pool or darts as much as he wanted to win football matches. He's such a fierce competitor."

Vardy ended up winning the Non-League National Game player of the year award in 2012. But just for once he didn't join his teammates on a boozy trip to the Grand National on the last day of the season when Wrexham drew 2-2 with Grimsby to confirm Fleetwood as champions.

"Vards stayed at home while we all went to Aintree," Atkinson told The Sun. "We were held 2-2 by Lincoln on Friday night and had to wait for Saturday's games to see if we had won the title. We were invited to the Grand National by the then Conference sponsors Blue Square and got paraded in the winners' enclosure when we were confirmed as champions — then got drunk.

"It was a rare occasion where Jamie wasn't involved."

It didn't take long for the other Fleetwood players to warm to Vardy either.

"I'd never heard of him," Gareth Seddon, who played alongside Vardy in a three-man attack for the side managed by Mickey Mellon, told The Guardian.

"At first some of the lads were like: 'Why have we signed this lad? From a few leagues below?' Then, in his first game, he was unbelievable. And we were just: 'That's the reason he signed!'

40

"I've never played with anyone as quick, I've been a professional for 18 years – he kind of glides across the pitch. He's got nothing to him, yet he was aggressive, and has energy. We did the bleep test and he just went and went and went. We were like: 'Frigging hell!'

"When he went full-time training – because we were full-time at Fleetwood – he just came on unbelievably. Every time he ran through on goal we just knew that he was not going to miss. It was unreal. He just never missed."

His other strike partner, Andy Mangan, said: "One thing I know is that if we wouldn't have had Jamie Vardy that year there is not a chance we would have won that league. I scored 24 and he scored 34 and set up most of mine but the biggest thing you can say about him, the biggest inspiration, is that he fears nothing.

"He could play against John Terry or whoever - he doesn't care. He just goes out there and plays his football."

"When Jamie first came in, no one really knew much about him," said Jamie Milligan, who also played with Vardy at Fleetwood. "We'd heard he had scored quite a lot of goals for Halifax and Stocksbridge, but no one was sure whether he could do it at this level.

"But as soon as he came in, he made a mark with his technique, his work rate and his goals, and straightaway everyone took a liking to him. His work rate rubbed off on everyone else. Jamie is no different now from how he was at Fleetwood. He was fearless. He got on with everyone. He was always up for a laugh. But when it came to training, he was focused.

"There were games in which he scored from near the halfway line," Milligan told Bleacher Report. "Some of the games we were struggling in, we could rely on him. We had a good squad, but he was a lot better than everyone else.

"Everyone got on with Jamie. I text him now and again. He keeps in touch with a few of the lads at Fleetwood. He will never get ideas above his station."

Vardy won the Conference title with Fleetwood in 2012 – but training could be bracing.

"I had to do the naked run as a forfeit for something silly like being late into training," he said. "It wasn't the best time because it was around winter and it's freezing up in Fleetwood. I sprinted all the way. The lads were on the balcony giving me wolf whistles. Thank God it wasn't captured on camera."

Vardy scored 34 goals in 36 games during his one season at Highbury, again boosting the club's promotion hopes.

In many ways, it was a baptism of fire. He remembered one game against Luton: "Abuse comes with the territory of being a footballer but it was just carnage that afternoon. We were winning 1-0 at half-time, I'd dinked the keeper and obviously celebrated a bit mad.

"The fans were running after me and rocking the tunnel, and all their players were trying to get hold of one of our strikers. The police had to come into the dressing room and told us if we were going to start a riot they'd lock us up. We ended up getting out of there having won 2-1 but it was chaos."

"Off the field, Vardy was a great player to get to know," said Dave Riche. "The Fleetwood team at the time had a great sense of spirit and were in it together both on and off the field.

"Vardy loved his football, but he also loved to let his hair down with a beer and was just quite simply one of the lads. He would be quite happy sitting in the Golden Ball in the tiny village of Poulton le Fylde on the outskirts of Blackpool drinking a Crabbie's Ginger Ale after training and getting to know the local tradesmen, who he would often sort out with tickets to the game at the weekend.

"There was no arrogance, despite the headlines he was getting and he was doing his job week-in, week-out and scoring goals as Fleetwood went about their task of winning promotion to the Football League.

"His mates from back in Halifax used to come to watch him and one week came in fancy dress as Oompa Lumpa's while doing a conga around the terrace as their mate performed heroics on the pitch."

More and more scouts were shuffling into the ground in a long line each match day and Fleetwood was soon fending off seven figure offers.

"Our chairman, Andy Pilley, came to me and said we should have a punt on Vardy and I am happy to fund the fee. I remember questioning his logic at the time, I have to say, though we laugh about it now but I did think it was a lot of money at the time," said Fleetwood vice-chairman Phil Brown.

"We signed him on the Friday morning and he made his debut in the evening against York City. The manager was looking to bench him because he had only signed that day but the chairman put a touch of pressure on to start.

"I do recall, he might be a bit embarrassed about it, but because he was playing that night and after everything had been concluded and all the paperwork had been done, I organised for him to go to a local hotel in Blackpool to relax for a few hours and get something to eat.

"I remember his dad going: 'What, and we don't have to pay and we can have whatever we want to eat?' I said: 'Yes just help yourselves.' I remember his dad replying along the lines of 'Bloody hell son, we've done alright here'.

43

"He was someone to keep an eye on. He knew how to enjoy himself, shall we say. When he was off the leash, he was someone who would find himself in a little bit of bother. He knew how to let his hair down but he never caused us any real problems.

"We had had a huge amount of interest pretty much from the first few months he had started. His first goals were at Kettering Town and Barry Fry was there and said he was on his radar.

"From then on we were conscious of the interest because of the number of scouts that were coming to our games, the numbers of which were much higher than normal.

"One game, David Moyes was personally there, Mick McCarthy was there. We were getting some quite important people in the ground and it was obvious why they were there. Southampton were also very keen on him but geographically it didn't work for him."

The birth of Vardy's first daughter, Ella, knocked some of the rougher edges off the striker - that and the realisation that his stock was rapidly on the rise in football.

"When he started doing well and had his daughter it set him on a right path," said Seddon, who is now at Salford City. "He thought: 'I've got something to strive for here.' He realised that if he knuckled down he could make a life for him and his daughter.

"All the fans relate to him because he is a working-class lad – his upbringing, the kind of non-league mentality he's got. He's come from nothing, absolutely nothing. And he has worked his nuts off.

"A lot of it – it's not really for himself because he's one of those who does not care whether he's on two grand or two quid. But he's doing it for his family, his daughter and his girlfriend."

After one year at Fleetwood, the chairman's gamble didn't seem so outrageous. Nigel Pearson agreed terms to bring Vardy to Leicester City for £1 million.

Vardy was finally on his way…and he wasn't going to let anybody stop him now.

The away team in red lined up at the King Power Stadium boasting a strike force worth over £100 million. The hometown blues were pinning all their hopes on a 27-year-old former non-league forward making his first ever start in the English Premier League.

Leicester City's future success could perhaps be traced back to that September Sunday afternoon victory over the mighty Manchester United.

It was certainly the first time football fans outside the East Midlands became truly aware of the potent goal threat Jamie Vardy was becoming.

He scored one of the Foxes' goals in the stunning 5-3 victory but it was his overall performance that caught the eye in such stunning fashion. He laid on two assists and ran the United defence ragged to win two penalties after his team fell behind 3-1.

Quite simply, he ran, chased, blocked and harried the big-ticket players into submission.

Vardy himself earmarks that game as life-changing, perhaps for no other reason than it was the first time he realized that not only could he live with the best, he could surpass them.

He hadn't come through the youth academies being pampered and praised like so many of his contemporaries; quite the reverse, he'd been told more than once that he wasn't good enough to make the grade. Too short, too thin, too much trouble.

Yet there was, playing against the greatest club by a considerable margin in the Premier League era, and making them look like amateurs. He bulldozed his opponents with a finger-pointing, rip-roaring ferocity that surprised even the Leicester faithful.

"Frightening. Madness. Who would have thought that would ever have happened," Vardy said in an interview afterwards. "The whole day, no one gave us a chance before the game but to come away with a 5-3 victory the manner we did was just unbelievable.

"It was definitely my best game ever. I don't think anything can beat that. United's players didn't really speak afterwards. A lot of them were gutted about the game.

"I'm just a pest. That's all I've ever been. I don't know how to play any different. There is no sitting off, I just go straight at them. If you believe the United manager he said they'd done their research on us all week and had four books on us. So if he's doing that you'd expect other teams are doing exactly the same."

"The Cannon", as he's been nicknamed by teammates, wasn't yet firing on all barrels…but he'd served notice that he'd arrived.

However, as with pretty much everything else in this story, it didn't come easy even after Leicester paid a record £1 million fee for a non-league player to bring him to the KP Stadium from Fleetwood.

Manager Nigel Pearson was key in persuading Vardy to go for Leicester - then in the Championship - over other suitors for his signature. Pearson had been the captain of Vardy's hometown Sheffield Wednesday team and they shared a passion for the city that is home to the world's oldest football club.

But unlike at Fleetwood, where Vardy hit the ground running scoring right from the off, he struggled in his first season.

Jeers from the fans fed Vardy's insecurities. As confident as he was in his abilities there remained a part of his mind that put a cap on his aspirations. Was he good enough for the higher leagues? It was a question he couldn't avoid asking himself as his goals dwindled and dried up.

By the end of the 2012-13 season in the Championship he'd scored just 5 in 29 appearances.

He was so down he considered leaving the sport altogether. To have come so far and to have failed at what appeared to be the final hurdle was devastating. As a compromise, he asked Pearson to send him out on loan, presumably to a lower league club.

The manager refused. With assistant Craig Shakespeare, Pearson persuaded Vardy that he simply needed to adjust his game to the different demands of the Championship. It's not that he wasn't used to the physicality, it was simply more subtle and meted out by better, more skilful players than Vardy was used to dealing with.

It wouldn't take much to get it right, Pearson insisted.

"Yes I did nearly give up to be honest with you," Vardy would later tell BBC Late Kick Off Midlands. "But I had a few chats with the gaffer and they constantly told me I was good enough and they believed in me and stuck by me. I am glad to be showing the faith they showed in me on the pitch.

"I also know a lot of hard work has gone into it on my behalf as well as people believing in me."

The following season Vardy blossomed as his manager had hoped he would, scoring 16 times as Leicester were promoted to the top flight as champions.

"It was tough," Vardy recalled. "I came into a dressing room with a lot of big names in and I wasn't used to it whatsoever. It did take a lot to get used to and I obviously have now."

Once in the Premier League, Vardy again had to take a step back before heading forwards with all guns blazing. His goal total of five for the 2014-15 was the same as his confidence-sapping first with the club, but it was different for several important reasons and served as a springboard for the year that followed.

There was the importance of the goals for a start. The Manchester United display had got him noticed and although Leicester then went on a winless 13-match run that sunk them firmly to the bottom of the league, another Vardy goal was the crucial clincher against Burnley during the club's great escape that featured six wins in eight matches and guaranteed safety being achieved before the final day.

Even more importantly, Vardy had won over the fans with his do-or-die attacking. Supporters respond to players they know will be chasing every ball and every lost cause. Leicester's fans could always appreciate the silky skills of a player like Esteban Cambiasso, but because of where he came from, Vardy was one of them.

The end of the season was about relief as much as excitement. Vardy and his teammates had defied the odds and survived to fight another Premier League campaign.

The stage was set for Jamie Vardy to have a party.

The problem when Jamie Vardy first signed for Leicester City was that he was partying too much, according to a senior official at the club.

The striker had difficulty adjusting to the professional culture at a top club after years spent in the less focused changing rooms in the lower tiers where heavy drinking was more common.

Aiyawatt Srivaddhanaprabha, the Foxes vice chairman and son of the club's billionaire owner Vichai Srivaddhanaprabha, told a magazine in his native Thailand that Vardy would show up for training "still drunk."

He said the No. 9 didn't know what to do with his new-found wealth after moving to the club from non-League.

According to a story in The Independent, Vardy was said to have been out drinking "every single day" and was warned a number of times about his conduct.

"He went straight from the bottom to the Championship, which eventually led him to start drinking booze every single day. We had no idea what to do," Srivaddhanaprabha told A Day magazine in Thailand.

"I didn't even know about this until someone told me that he came to train while he was still drunk. So I went to talk to him myself, I asked 'do you wish to end your career like this? Do you want to stay here like this? We'll let your contract run out then release you. Don't expect a better career path.'

"He said he didn't know what to do with his life. He'd never earned such a large amount of money. So I asked him 'what's your dream?

"'How do you think your life should be? Just think carefully about what would you do for the club. I invested in you, do you have something in return?'

50

"After that he simply quit drinking and started working hard in training. His physicality wasn't as good as it is now.

"We know he had explosive acceleration, but we simply had no idea he could be this good.

"He's adapting, working on fitness training, he's turned into a new person. And that's better."

Leicester Captain Wes Morgan agreed that Vardy didn't fit right in. "It took him a while to adjust to the Championship and to find his feet," he said. "But ever since then he's been fantastic. The season we went up he was on fire and a constant problem for the teams facing us."

While he's matured off the field, Vardy doesn't think he's too different once the whistle blows. "Not really," he says. "I've always been energetic, fast... and a bit of a pest!"

Blackpool fans will argue that the great Stan Mortensen scored in 15 straight matches in the top tier in 1950-51, although the sequence was broken by games he was out with injury. In Spain, they will point to Lionel Messi's 21-game scoring streak for Barcelona in 2012-13 as an unmatchable achievement. For the handful left that can still remember, Sheffield United's Irish striker Jimmy Donne slotted home 12 goals in successive games in the old English First Division way back in 1931-2.

Few will take issue with the difficulty in hitting the net with any regularity in the modern day EPL, let alone in match after match.

Most of those who had done it in the past - with the notable exception of Ian Wright - were footballers with stellar pedigrees; soccer royalty like van Nistelrooy, Shearer, Sturridge and Henry.

Nobody, not even the man himself, would ever have believed the Premier League goalscoring streak record would be beaten by a mutt in an unfancied team who'd managed just five goals in his debut season in the top bracket.

But as late summer chilled towards winter in 2015, it was Jamie Vardy who scratched his name into the national consciousness and beyond. The previous season's player of the year Eden Hazard couldn't buy himself a goal; even the five Sergio Aguerro bagged for Manchester City in a single October game against Newcastle didn't hold the footballing public's attention for long.

Everybody, whatever their club colours, wanted to know if Vardy could carry on "The Streak."

Vardy would never claim to be a great public speaker. His interviews are littered with the usual footballers clichés - taking it one game at a time, it's not about me; it's all about the team, the record's not on my mind. But people didn't want to hear him speak, they wanted to see him play, they wanted to see him score - just not against their team.

As belief grew through the autumn so did Vardy's profile. Now he was on England manager Roy Hodgson's radar, as well.

Friends say Vardy's ability to remain calm in the whirlwind of expectation was largely due to his demeanour off the pitch. He'd seen enough of the ups and downs of the game to understand the football gods were fickle. He played his heart out every match, so much so that he can hardly walk the following day, but once the final whistle has gone he retains his equanimity whatever the result. He's not tormenting himself for days after a defeat.

Even as the pressure mounted with the record in touching distance, Vardy didn't behave any differently in training, at home...or during games. He knew his chances would come. If he missed, he'd try again. It was a prosaic approach but, in the circumstances, extremely effective. Strikers on form don't question; they shoot.

On the night before the potential record-making game, he felt no nerves. "No nerves, nothing," he said. If the whole country was excited about the possibilities, Vardy was taking it in his stride.

It was appropriate that Manchester United was the opposition for the 11th game. Vardy's hard-charging performance against United the previous year was the foundation for his later exploits and Dutchman Ruud van Nistelrooy held the record of ten successive strikes for the 13-time Premier League champions since the 2003 season.

The goal, when it came, was pure Jamie Vardy - and pure Leicester City.

Goalkeeper Kasper Schmeichel - son of United's legendary keeper Peter - caught the ball from a corner and immediately launched the counter attack by releasing the ball to Austrian fullback Christian Fuchs on the right of his penalty box.

As soon as Vardy saw Fuchs had the ball he was off. Ashley Young, no slough himself, tried to slow the striker by twice pulling at his shirt but his cheating was in vain. Vardy crossed the halfway line and made a beeline for Manchester's penalty area, pointing to the green space behind opposing defender Matteo Darmian.

As soon as Fuchs released the ball, Vardy put his foot on the accelerator and raced past Darmian. Bearing down on keeper David de Gea he knew exactly what he was going to do. He slipped the ball around the advancing de Gea, low and precise inside the far post.

Three players, two passes, one goal.

Fast, incisive, clinical.

Claudio Ranieri had set the team two goals before the game - to win and to help Vardy snag the record. The final 1-1 result meant the afternoon hadn't been entirely successful, but the manager was no less extravagant with his praise afterwards.

"Jamie made the record, it is fantastic for us," he said. "Five years ago he played in non-league, it is difficult to grow up so quickly and this fantastic man is not only our goal scorer but he presses, he works hard, he is important."

Manchester United boss Louis van Gaal also praised Vardy's "amazing and fantastic" feat, saying: "The goal he scored is also amazing because it is not so easy. I can say our organisation is bad but he is provoking that also. It is a fantastic record to have, 11 matches in a row. Not many players will do that."

Vardy was typically understated. "The record was not in my mind, it would have affected my performance and the team's, and that's the last thing I wanted to do.

"I can think about it when I am home but as soon as I cross the white line all I should be concentrating on is my football.

"That's what I have been doing and exactly what I will continue to do."

The streak had begun on August 29 with Leicester in third place and at one point after the humbling 2-5 loss to Arsenal almost a month later the club had slipped to 6th and the naysayers were gleefully predicting a steady slide back down the table.

But Vardy's goals were proof of the growing belief across the team that their success wasn't a fluke.

By the time Vardy hit his historic strike against United on November 28, Leicester City was in first place and determined to stay on top.

HOW HE DID IT

Four goals after the 80th minute, three from the penalty spot and some while bones were broken, here's a look at how Vardy's magnificent streak took place, courtesy of BBC Sport.

29 August: Bournemouth 1-1 Leicester

It all started on the South Coast as Vardy was fouled in the box and picked himself up to smash in a late penalty and rescue a point. It preserved Leicester's unbeaten start to the season after four games.

League position: 3rd

13 September: Leicester 3-2 Aston Villa

Leicester made a stunning second-half comeback from 2-0 down to beat Villa, with Vardy netting the equaliser in the 82nd minute from close range

League position: 2nd

19 September: Stoke 2-2 Leicester

Once again, Leicester came from behind to get something out of a game. Could Vardy do it on a sunny Saturday afternoon at Stoke? You bet he could, holding off the chasing defence to claim the equaliser.

League position: 3rd

26 September: Leicester 2-5 Arsenal

Claudio Ranieri's side suffered their first defeat of the season after being demolished by an Alexis Sanchez hat-trick, but Vardy managed to grab both his side's goals, including an 89th-minute consolation.

League position: 6th

3 October: Norwich 1-2 Leicester

Vardy struck another penalty as Leicester got back to winning ways, despite manager Ranieri revealing the striker was playing with two broken bones in his wrist suffered against Villa. He wouldn't get the breaks repaired until after the European Championships the following summer.

League position: 4th

17 October: Southampton 2-2 Leicester

Two goals down again. No problem when you have Vardy in your side. The former non-league frontman pulled a goal back with a header and blasted home in injury time to tie it up.

League position: 5th

24 October: Leicester 1-0 Crystal Palace

Vardy is known for his all-action style of play, but has he got the technical ability in his game? Of course, he has. He showed composure by nicking the ball over the goalkeeper and slotting in the winner against Palace.

League position: 5th

31 October: West Brom 2-3 Leicester

Vardy's run almost came to an end against the Baggies when he went down injured - but after treatment from the physio he returned to the pitch and netted his side's third goal - his favourite from the 11 games.

League position: 3rd

7 November: Leicester 2-1 Watford

Another injury scare, this time going down holding his groin. Nothing was going to stop Vardy on his mission, though, and the lad can hold his nerve. Another from the spot, another win for Leicester.

League position: 3rd

21 November: Newcastle 0-3 Leicester

Vardy joined Ruud van Nistelrooy by scoring in 10 straight games after netting just before half-time. Better news was to come as Manchester City and Arsenal lost, leaving Leicester top of the table.

League position: 1st

28 November: Leicester 1-1 Manchester United

He's done it!! Vardy becomes a record-breaker, getting on the end of Christian Fuchs' through ball and slotting past David de Gea. The new ace marksman celebrated in style, pointing to his chest, and shouting 'all mine, all mine'.

League position: 2nd

WHO HE BEAT (in the Premier League era)

Jamie Vardy (Leicester City) - 10 games - 2015

Ruud van Nistelrooy (Manchester United) - 10 games - 2003

Ruud van Nistelrooy (Manchester United) - 8 games - 2002

Daniel Sturridge (Liverpool) - 8 games - 2014

Mark Stein (Chelsea), Ian Wright, Emmanuel Adebayor and Thierry Henry (Arsenal), Alan Shearer (Newcastle) - all 7 games

HOW THE STREAK COMPARES IN EUROPE

Jamie Vardy still has a way to go to match the record holders in some of Europe's other top six domestic leagues. Here's the UEFA.COM list of Europe's other leading serial goal scorers:

Portugal: Fernando Peyroteo (Sporting CP) – 10

One of the 'Cinco Violinos' (Five Violins) who helped Sporting dominate Portuguese football in the 1940s, Peyroteo announced himself in style in 1937/38, registering in each of the final ten games of his debut campaign. Even more remarkable was the fact he struck 31 times across those ten matches. The Angolan-born attacker notched more goals than games played in all 12 seasons with the Leões, hitting a Sporting-record 297 goals before retiring at 31.

Italy: Gabriel Batistuta (Fiorentina) – 11

"I have made Italian football history," beamed Batistuta after netting in Fiorentina's 2-2 draw with Sampdoria on 27 November 1994. "Maybe in 20 years you will come to my home in Reconquista [Argentina] because there will be a new Batistuta trying to beat my record." It has not happened yet. "I'm happy because nobody remembered my record until today," said ex-Bologna front man Ezio Pascutti, who had registered in ten straight games in 1962.

France: Serge Masnaghetti (Valenciennes) – 13

There is no official record in France for goals in consecutive fixtures, but Masnaghetti is commonly regarded as having set the mark in 1962/63. That season brought 35 of his 111 career goals, which remains a club record. The great Jean-Pierre Papin would later feel the force of Masnaghetti when he suggested that "scoring was easier in the old days". "Do you think defenders let me go because I was a nice guy?" smirked Masnaghetti.

Germany: Gerd Müller (Bayern München) – 16

Between 27 September 1969 and 3 March 1970 the master poacher found the target in 16 Bundesliga games running. Not a prime physical specimen – Bayern coach Zlatko Čajkovski affectionately called him 'kleines dickes Müller' (little fat Müller) – his goalscoring remains the stuff of legend. "Bayern have Gerd Müller to thank for what the club has become," said Franz Beckenbauer. "Without Gerd's goals, we'd still be sitting in a wood hut at Säbener Strasse [training ground]."

Spain: Lionel Messi (Barcelona) – 21

Carrying a thigh injury, Messi began Barcelona's 34th Liga match of 2012/13 on the bench against Betis. With his side struggling to overcome the challenge of the stubborn visitors, the Argentina ace was summoned and duly delivered – notching his 45th and 46th top-flight goals of the season to extend his Liga scoring streak to 21 games in a row. Atlético Madrid ended the run next time out but by then the previous record of ten set by Barcelona's Ronaldo in 1996/97 was long forgotten.

OTHER EPL SERIAL STRIKERS

Arsenal (7) Henry, Wright, Adebayor

Aston Villa (5)   Dublin

Bournemouth   (2) Murray, Wilson

Chelsea (7) Stein

Crystal Palace   (5) Shipperley

Everton (5) Ferguson

Leicester City (11) Vardy

Liverpool (8) Sturridge

Manchester City (5) Aguero (three times)

Manchester United (10) van Nistelrooy

Newcastle United (7) Shearer

Norwich City (3) Ashton, Holt, Morison,

Sutton (8 runs in total)

Southampton (6) Beattie

Stoke City (3) Crouch, Etherington,

Fuller, Jones, Odemwingie

Sunderland (5) Bent, Fletcher

Swansea City (4) Graham, Michu, Gomis

Tottenham Hotspur (5) Sheringham, Keane (x3),

Van der Vaart, Bale

Watford (3) Ngonge, Smart, Deeney

61

West Brom (5) Odemwingie

West Ham United (6) Sakho

Jamie Vardy insists he never gets nervous - but even the cold-blooded striker must have felt a few jitters as he watched his bride walk down the aisle towards him at his fairytale castle wedding on May 25, 2016.

The striker was reunited with his old Leicester City strike partner, David Nugent, now with newly promoted Middlesborough, who was his choice as best man. His current teammates were also on hand to cheer Vardy on at the romantic wedding at historic Peckforton Castle in Cheshire.

Stunning in white, bride Rebekah "Becky" Nicholson walked down the aisle in a dress by Knightsbridge-based Caroline Castigliano, whose gowns range from £4,000 to £7,000.

It was the culmination of an incredible year for the Premier League sharpshooter - with the Euros still to come a few weeks later.

In fact, the early June wedding date the couple had pencilled in had to be brought back a couple of weeks - and held midweek - because it was originally going to clash with the start of the championships.

Other footballers married at Peckforton Castle include Rio Ferdinand, Phil Bardsley, Fabrice Muamba, Wes Brown and Alan Smith. Guests at the castle can be greeted by a golden eagle while wedding rings — on request — are delivered by a barn owl to the groom's hands.

On the Vardy's big day, guests included celebrities like rapper Tinchy, Westlife singer Shane Filan, 2013 X Factor winner Sam Bailey and Kasabian's Serge Pizzorno.

There was one shadow of sadness over the previous 12 months, just when it seemed like all of family man Vardy's dreams were coming true one at a time.

In all that time, the striker had been estranged from his parents because of a bitter dispute over his then fiancée.

He wasn't on speaking terms with his mum, Lisa, dad Phil or his maternal grandparents who reportedly blamed "that woman" for the rift.

Speaking to The Sun newspaper from his terraced home in Sheffield in November 2015, Phil Vardy said: "We don't talk to Jamie. I have given 22 years of life to get him where he is today and I've had it all thrown back in my face."

"We won't be going to the wedding," he added, fighting back tears. "It's been going on for a year now since she came on the scene."

Referring to his son's brush with the law when Vardy was forced to wear an electronic ankle tag even while playing for his non-league club, Phil continued: "When Jamie was in trouble before, it was me who was travelling all around the country getting him home in time for his curfew. It's a real shame and very sad.

"I don't have anything to do with him any more and, as you can tell, it really upsets me."

Vardy's grandfather Gerald Clewes, who is in his seventies, also claimed Becky was the reason for the family split without saying why.

"As far as the football goes we are very proud of Jamie. But it's a bit awkward as we never see him any more," he said. "It's a real shame. I don't go to his games any more. I have never been to Leicester."

Asked by The Sun if Vardy was on good terms with his mother, Clewes added: "No — not any more. You should look into that woman he's got."

64

Vardy first met the sultry brunette in a nightclub in January 2014, and she was later asked to organise a party for an up-and-coming football star as part of her job as an events planner.

At that time, Becky already had two children, Megan and Taylor, from previous relationships and Vardy had a little girl, Ella, with ex-girlfriend Emma Daggett.

Vardy and Becky also now have a daughter Sofia, who was born in December, 2014.

"It certainly wasn't an immediate attraction when I did meet him," Becky recalled in an interview. "It took a lot of persuasion on Jamie's part to get me remotely interested."

However, as we now know, Vardy is not one to give up easily.

"I must have said, 'No thanks I'm not interested' for the best part of two months - he was very persistent though, asking me to go for a drink.

"It's just the same as with his career – he never gives up! But he won me over or we wouldn't be sat here now.

"When we did go for a drink he made me laugh a lot, but mainly I thought, 'This guy's insane!'"

It hasn't been an easy ride for her as her partner's fame rocketed in the time they've been together, bringing with it unkind stories about Becky's past relationships and portrayals of her as a football WAG.

There were reports of a fling with 'Strictly Come Dancing' star Peter Andre following the breakdown of her first marriage in 2001. Although she was said to have been attracted by his "great muscles" the tryst supposedly lasted just five minutes and the young model was supposedly strictly underwhelmed.

Another tabloid story alleged she told her ex-boyfriend, non-league footballer Luke Foster, that she was leaving him because she was "upgrading" to the Premier League star, a claim she adamantly denied.

Foster, a former Oxford United defender, had a son with Becky in 2010, but their relationship was reportedly already crumbling. Friends said Foster helped Becky get a job at the Viper Rooms nightclub in Sheffield, where she first met Vardy and was later commissioned to organise his birthday party.

Becky dismisses the gossip. "Fortunately I've got quite a thick skin," she said in the interview. "I understand that there are a lot of nice things said too and they do outweigh negative things – so I try just let hurtful things wash over me."

The couple are almost inseparable when Vardy's away from the game. They are happy to spend nights at home at their mansion in Melton Mowbray, Leicestershire, rather than going out on the town.

"You have to take the good with the bad and it's 99% good so I can't complain about the 1% bad.... I'd be mad to!"

Becky, who's five years older than Vardy, told The Mirror: "He's shown you should never give up on your dreams, whatever they might be."

She said in a TV interview that the past 12 months had been "surreal."

"Credit where credit's due - I'm so proud of him," she continued. "From a football perspective he hasn't changed much but from a personal perspective he's definitely matured - not that I'm saying he was a little kid before. There's definitely been an improvement.

"I never in a million years doubted he'd do it."

When she discusses Vardy's maturity, she's referring in part to his skills as a dad.

66

"He's amazing with all of them - a fantastic dad. He'll walk in from training absolutely knackered and the first thing he'll do is ask them how they are," said Becky. "What you see is what you get with Jamie - he's the calmest person. Win or lose he's the same."

Vardy's ex-girlfriend, Emma Daggett, hasn't been so complimentary about him in the press. She met the striker in 2008 when she was 20 and he was just 22 and still playing for non-league Stocksbridge Park Steels. They spit a couple of years later following Ella's birth and their daughter now lives with her mum, an admin worker, in the north of England.

"It's difficult," Emma was quoted as saying to The Sun on Sunday in April, 2016. "He's never really around so he can't really commit to her," she said of Ella. "He doesn't see her very often. It's maybe once a month."

Back home in Leicestershire, Vardy says his bad boy days are far behind him.

But once the kids are tucked up in bed, that doesn't necessarily mean Vardy's heard the last from his teammates.

"A few of the lads have PS4 and we play 'Call of Duty' between us. If we're not going out together you'll see us on the PS4."

"You'd stay on it all night," interrupted Becky, smiling.

On stories painting her as a football WAG, she insists: "It's not me and I'll never be like that. You won't see me turning up to the gym with a full face of make-up and my hair done. I'm just a normal person.

"My other half happens to play football for a living but that won't change me. I wear Top Shop practically every day; labels make no difference to me. It's not about money, it's about what you feel comfortable in."

She said of down-to-earth Vardy: "He's the least extravagant person you could ever meet and there's nothing materialistic about him at all."

That maybe why Becky played a trick on Vardy at their wedding, serving up Pot Noodles to the guests while joking that they were the only thing her new husband could cook (they were then served up with the proper sit-down meal!)

Looking ahead, Becky added: "Who knows what the perfect Hollywood ending is going to be? We haven't got a clue where the end will be; we're still right in the middle of the fairy-tale.

"I'd like another baby. I'd love another boy. I'm not sure how Jamie will feel. But as long as we're happy, and the kids are happy, that's our goal. We're securing their future. That's the happy ending for us."

Although he changed the wedding date three times because of his England commitments, Vardy's nuptials still came bang in the middle of the national side's preparations for the 2016 Euros. The groom was given special dispensation from manager Roy Hodgson to get hitched while club and international teammate Danny Drinkwater was only allowed out of the England camp for the ceremony and had to head back before the reception.

Vardy kept his word to have "a very quiet night" and was back on England duty a couple of days later. Hodgson said he had faith in Vardy behaving appropriately. "I'm really not concerned," he said before the wedding. "I hope he will be sensible and I believe he will be sensible.

"I know he really is desperate to be selected to go to the Euros and do a good job so I'm pretty confident when I see him on Saturday morning he will be fine. By all means feel free to ask if he intends to let down his hair and do some stupid things after the wedding — and if the answer is yes, feel free to batter him."

The England boss's faith was justified. Vardy turned up back in camp ready to go. His season wasn't yet over. He was about to star on his biggest stage yet competing with some of the best players in the world.

While he was manager at West Bromwich Albion, Roy Hodgson made the short trip east to watch a much-touted non-league striker turn out at Kidderminster Harriers.

He decided to pass on the player, who was unproven at the higher level. Just a few years later he was picking that same player, Jamie Vardy, to lead his line in the 2016 European Championships in France.

"I got told before the Kidderminster game he was there," recalled Vardy later. "We were live on television but I think it was a bad game for him to come to. It was very windy and the pitch was like sand dunes. There were bobbles everywhere but we won the game.

"I never thought I could make it to the Premier League. I just wanted to keep improving as much as I could and see where that got me."

His first cap came before he'd really hit his stride in the Premier League. Hodgson remembered the wiry hitman and was impressed enough with the role he'd played in Leicester's survival battle to call him into the squad at the end of the 2014-15 season.

He made his debut on 7 June in the goalless draw against the Republic of Ireland at the Aviva Stadium in Dublin, replacing captain Wayne Rooney for the final 15 minutes.

He did well enough to again called up to the England squad on August 30, 2015 for the games against San Marino and Switzerland in the UEFA Euro 2016 qualifying round, making the starting line-up as England ran out 6–0 winners against San Marino in Serravalle six days later.

By the time he next pulled on an England shirt he was the hottest striker in the country along with Tottenham's Harry Kane, and the script unfolded with the same plot Vardy had been following all year.

He scored his first international goal on March 26, 2016, equalising with a flamboyant back heel from Nathaniel Clyne's cross, while playing as a substitute in a 3–2 away win against Germany.

Gordon Taylor, chief executive of the English footballers' trades union, the Professional Footballers' Association since 1981, marvelled along with the rest of the country, saying afterwards: "If the likes of Pele, Messi or Ronaldo had scored that then everybody would talk about it as one of the best ever but it was an absolute inspirational marvellous goal. To come from a lad who just a few years ago was rattling away at Stocksbridge Steels it's the stuff that dreams are made of."

Three days later, Vardy scored again, the opening goal in a 2–1 defeat to the Netherlands at Wembley.

Some jokers suggested the striker's outrageous camouflage boots played a part. They were certainly a sign of Vardy's comfort in his new surroundings - he would never have got away with wearing them in the old days versus Southport!

Vardy wasn't about to let his impending nuptials get in the way of his England Euros preparations and he started alongside Kane for the friendly against Turkey on May 22, winning a penalty and scoring the late goal that clinched a 2-1 victory.

The classic poacher's strike made it three goals in three games for his country but the game wasn't without controversy with TV pundits questioning an earlier penalty won by Vardy - both former Arsenal stars Lee Dixon and Ian Wright suggesting that he dived.

Vardy was running at full place into the opposition penalty box when he got the slightest of touches and went down. Harry Kane missed the penalty, making the inquests redundant, but the incident raised questions about Vardy's gamesmanship.

Not that the man himself was worried. He was on another scoring streak!

There are some who say Jamie Vardy shouldn't have even been playing for Leicester City after he was caught on video racially abusing a fellow gambler in a casino.

The footage, reportedly shot in the early hours of July 26, 2015, appears to show an aggressive Vardy using the term "Jap" on three occasions.

Following on the heels of a sex scandal that would have huge ramifications for the club, it couldn't have come at a worse time. Leicester had sacked three players in June 2015 after they filmed themselves taking part in a racist orgy during a goodwill visit to Bangkok.

But Ranieri and the club's owners - the Srivaddhanaprabha family from Thailand - resisted demands to fire their star striker, instead fining him a week's wages (approximately £40,000) and sending him on a diversity awareness programme.

Vardy also issued a grovelling apology over his use of the word "Jap", short for Japanese, which has been considered a derogatory racial term since World War II. "I wholeheartedly apologise for any offence I've caused," he said. "It was a regrettable error in judgment I take full responsibility for and I accept my behaviour was not up to what's expected of me."

The player's supporters, Gary Lineker among them, may have argued it was a "stupid" mistake and there was no racist intent, but Vardy's abhorrent insults undoubtedly left a nasty taste in the mouths of many who otherwise would have celebrated his ensuing achievements without the racism asterisk.

In the video, Vardy is seen sitting next to then fiancee Becky Nicholson. He was playing high stakes poker at about 1.20am when he reportedly thought a middle-aged man standing behind him was looking at his cards.

Vardy can be seen gesticulating and shouting, "Yo Jap, walk on."

He points and says: "Jap. Yo Jap. Walk on. Walk on . . . oi, walk on. Yeah you . . . Jap. Walk on."

"It was awful," a witness was quoted as saying. "He then said, 'Away'. His girlfriend says to the man, 'You've been looking at his cards'. They rowed for a couple of minutes and then the other guy eventually walked off."

Just minutes later Vardy is alleged to have become involved in another angry dispute when a customer pointed out to him that watching a poker table is allowed, as long as you make no comment on the hand being played.

The striker is said to have become angry and asked the customer "outside" to settle the argument. Leicester's Belgian defender Ritchie De LaetDe Laet is then said to have held Vardy in a headlock to prevent him going.

De Laet and a third player, David Nugent, were also at the casino but there was never a suggestion they did anything inappropriate. Both apparently tried to calm Vardy down.

An eyewitness was quoted as telling The Sun: "He behaved like an absolute animal, it was appalling. The other guy was a man of East Asian appearance. He looked shocked by what happened.

"As an England international he should know that eyes are going to be on him when he goes out, but he acted just like a football thug."

The anti-racism campaign group 'Kick It Out' said the incident "cast a shadow" over the start of the new season.

74

"It is disappointing that the opening weekend of the season, which should be a time of celebration, has been overshadowed by these allegations," said 'Kick It Out' director Roisin Wood.

"Footballers, no matter the level they play at, are role models on and off the field and their behaviour can impact millions of fans across the country.

"If these allegations are proven, we would consider it to be a serious matter and would expect the club to conduct a swift and thorough investigation. We have contacted the club and await their response."

Few then believed Vardy was to become such a high profile part of the new 2015-16 campaign. If anything, some argued, Vardy's subsequent success made it all the more important for him to properly make amends.

Daily Telegraph writer Jonathan Liew was among those who thought Vardy's punishment was woefully insufficient. Immediately after the striker scored in his record-breaking 11th game in November 2015 the journalist tweeted: "Well done Jamie Vardy, you massive racist."

He followed this up with a more detailed post on Facebook explaining his reasons: "My view is this: racists should be pariahs. They should be punished with the full fist of the law and beaten down by the crushing yoke of public opinion. They should be out of a job. They should be out of friends. They should have to get on their knees and beg us all for forgiveness.

"Vardy should be out of work right now. But seeing as he's not, he can use his platform. He should be speaking out against racism at every opportunity. He should be working tirelessly with charities, doing talks in schools, educating young players on diversity and tolerance.

"And he should still be apologising. Every time there's a camera on him or a microphone in front of his face, he should start by expressing his remorse for what he did and telling us how he's putting things right."

It was a sobering lesson for Vardy that life both on and off the pitch in the Premier League is very different from the lower tiers of English football.

His friends point to his close friendships with his teammates of all races - among them Japanese international Shinji Okazaki - as proof that Vardy is not a racist and hadn't meant to be racially insensitive that night at the casino.

But the world is watching now. It's hard to see how any kind of repeat of this kind of behaviour would be tolerated, no matter how many goals Vardy scores.

This was supposed to be Nigel Pearson's team.

It was Pearson who brought the core of Leicester City's squad to the King Power and led the rock bottom club to its great escape from relegation at the end of the 2014-15 season, winning seven of the final nine games.

Without Pearson there may not have been a Jamie Vardy. It was, after all, the Sheffield connection the men shared that persuaded the frontman to sign for the former Wednesday skipper in the first place.

Who knows if the Nottingham-born former pro's more direct methods would have been as effective as his successor's sophisticated eccentricity in making the impossible dream of becoming Premier League champions a reality?

His relationship with the club's Thai owners was certainly strained, never a springboard for success in any business.

But a pre-season "goodwill tour" to Thailand would push that relationship to breaking point with three of Leicester's trainee players - one of them Pearson's son, James - embroiled in an embarrassing scandal over a <u>racist sex tape</u>.

The young Pearson, a defender then aged 22, striker Tom Hopper, who was 21, and 22-year-old goalkeeper Adam Smith were all sent home from the June 2015 club trip after they were seen committing sex acts with three Thai girls, in footage obtained by the Sunday Mirror.

The naked players were filmed hurling insults during the clip, shared among friends back in the UK, with one woman called a 'slit eye' and another taunted as "minging."

The depraved sex session reportedly involved as many as 10 Thai women. According to the newspaper, the players can be heard laughing throughout. At one stage after the initial insults have been made, one is heard off-camera shouting at Hopper: "Oi Hops, I'll swap you." Later, one of the men is caught saying, "Come on...you slit-eye."

At one stage, the Sunday Mirror claimed the three players watched the women indulging in lesbian sex acts. The clip reportedly ends with Hopper and Pearson, the development squad captain, giving one another high fives.

After an internal probe, all three players were axed. "The decision follows the conclusion of an internal investigation and disciplinary proceedings, as a consequence of events that took place during the Club's end-of-season goodwill tour of Thailand," the club said in a statement.

"Leicester City Football Club is acutely aware of its position, and that of its players, as a representative of the city of Leicester, the Premier League, the Football Association and the Club's supporters. It is committed to promoting a positive message of community and family values and equality, and to upholding the standards expected of a Club with its history, tradition and aspirations."

The incident was particularly humiliating for Leicester's billionaire Thai owners. Vichai Srivaddhanaprabha and his son Aiyawatt, known as Top, paid for the annual trip which was designed to promote the club and boost football's popularity in the Far East.

A few weeks later, the manager was out, as well.

He was dismissed at the beginning of July 2015 with the club claiming there were "fundamental differences in perspective" between manager and board.

Despite Pearson's unquestioned achievements in keeping Leicester up, he had already been involved in a series of high profile incidents that rubbed the image-conscious owners the wrong way.

In December 2014, he appeared to tell a supporter who was heckling him that he should f*** off and die.'

He managed to survive the inquest into that and there was a farcical situation the following February when he was caught on camera grappling on the touchline with Crystal Palace midfielder James McArthur.

Upset with his manager's mercurial behaviour, the club's owner Vichai Srivaddhanaprabha, who was at the 1-0 home defeat, fired Pearson, only to reinstate him over the phone after being persuaded by his son that there was no realistic replacement.

"In an ideal world I would rather the story not be out there but it is out there and I have to deal with it," Pearson was reported to have said at the time. "But I have loyalties to the people I work for and to my staff and the players and that is more important than trying to clarify things.
I like the people I work alongside to be loyal and I like to show them loyalty back.
I have good working relationship with them and a very good personal relationship as well.

"The discussions I have will remain in house. I am not a believer in sharing too much confidential information. I will continue to do my job and I am very happy to do my job."

Pearson then called popular former Foxes striker Gary Lineker a "fountain of knowledge" for making a "mountain out of a molehill" on Match Of The Day about his touchline spat.

Lineker responded on Twitter: "If I was I'd tell you that he was sacked by one of the owners' family and reinstated by another, but then I'm not."

Pearson wouldn't let things lie, hitting back with a personal attack on Lineker, who put money in a controversial tax break scheme, saying: "I don't care what they think of me, I pay my tax bills."

In April, he was in the headlines for the wrong reasons again when he launched into a bizarre rant during a press conference, branding one journalist an ostrich before storming out.

Complaining that his team had been unfairly criticised, he sought to disparage agency sports writer Ian Baker. The exchange went something like this:

BAKER: What criticism are you talking about?

PEARSON: Have you been on holiday for six months? Have you been away for six months?

BAKER: I am not quite sure what specific criticism you are referring to?

PEARSON: I think you must have been either head in the clouds or away on holiday or reporting on a different team because if you don't know the answer to that question your question is absolutely unbelievable the fact you do not understand where I am coming from. If you don't know the answer to that question then I think you are an ostrich. Your head must be in the sand. Is your head in the sand? Are you flexible enough to get your head in the sand? My suspicion would be no.

BAKER: Probably not.

PEARSON: I can, you can't. You can't. Listen you have been here often enough and for you to ask that question, you are either being very, very silly or you are being absolutely stupid, one of the two because for you to ask that question, I am sorry son, you are daft.

80

BAKER: There hasn't been much harsh criticism of the players.

PEARSON: You are wrong. No, you are wrong. You have been in here, I know you have so don't give that crap with me, please don't give that crap with me. I will smile at you because I can afford to smile at you. Now do you want to ask a different question or do you want to ask it differently. Come on, ask it. Ask it or are you not capable?

BAKER: I just don't know what you, erm…

PEARSON: You don't know, what erm?

BAKER: I don't know how you've taken that question.

PEARSON: Well you must be very stupid. I'm sorry.

The sex scandal was the final straw. The media speculated that the decision to sack the manager after his son's involvement in the orgy came as a result of the owners' deteriorating relationship with Pearson.

BBC Sport's Pat Murphy reported the firing was "definitely not a football issue."

"Religion is very important to the Srivaddhanaprabha family and observers have often see Buddhist monks in and around the players area after a home match - as guests of the owners," he wrote. "So clearly integrity and humility are important issues and that something like this happened on the 'goodwill tour' of their homeland would be very hard for them to accept.

"But fundamentally, should the sins of the son be visited on the father?" he added. "In footballing terms this is very harsh on Pearson."

His departure would become all the more cruel as he watched the side he built rise up the table under its new Italian manager and win it all, including Manager of the Year for Claudio Ranieri.

The name of Nigel Pearson, as vital as his signings were to the make-up of the Premier League winning team, would end the season as a mere foot-note in the club's rise from the ashes of near-relegation.

As the season progressed and Leicester City refused to fall away, the pundits kept looking for reasons to suggest the team of misfits, cast-offs and journeymen could go all the way.

They really couldn't find one.

Good team spirit is all very well but enough to win arguably the toughest sports league in the world? Probably not.

Vardy's goals were certainly a huge plus but the only established world class player Leicester had, Esteban Cambiasso, quit one month before the start of the season to play in the Champions League with Olympiacos. The former Real Madrid and Inter Milan midfielder - Leicester's 2014-15 Player of the Year - was clearly among those who didn't have a lot of faith in the club's future under Ranieri (he must be kicking himself now!). To be fair, Leicester's cheerleader, Gary Lineker, didn't think much of the appointment at the outset either.

Leicester started the season without a single recognised star player and a simple target - survival in the Premier League. It ended the victorious campaign the following May with a whole team of heroes , with a handful of them being chased by the likes of Barcelona, Real Madrid and PSG.

Time will tell whether 2015-16 was like lightning in a bottle. Chemistry, destiny, plain hard work; the experts are still trying to put a finger on a team that defied all the odds.

For most of the team it was a long, roundabout route to the top. See how they all got to there:

KASPER SCHMEICHEL

The Denmark international was in terrific form all season, keeping 15 clean sheets and guarding his area with the calm assurance of a seasoned professional. He played in all 38 games.

He's known success before, of course, but it was all achieved by his father, Peter, who won five titles with Manchester United and was one of the most formidable shot stoppers of his generation.

Kasper's route to the top, in common with many of his teammates, was much longer.

The 6'1" keeper may have dreamed as a boy of emulating his father but after sliding down the leagues following his release from Manchester City in 2009 after just nine first team appearances he must have thought his chance was lost.

While at Eastlands, he bounced around on loan between Darlington, Bury, Falkirk, Cardiff and Coventry before finally being bought by ex-England boss Sven Goran Eriksson, who took him to Notts County.

After helping County to a League 2 trophy, he moved on a free transfer to Leeds United, making 41 appearances before being sold to Leicester City in June 2011.

It's been a remarkable rollercoaster ride for the man who first held the Premier League trophy as a 12-year-old boy celebrating on the pitch at Old Trafford after his father's United had won the title in 1999, as the first step towards a famous treble.

"That is the just the beauty of football, anything can happen," Kasper told Sky Sports. Even emerging from the shadow of a goalkeeping great.

CHRISTIAN FUCHS

The Austrian team captain joined Leicester on a free transfer in the summer of 2015 after spending four years at German Bundesliga giants Schalke 04.

Persuaded to come to England by Nigel Pearson, he learned the manager had been axed just days before he was due to fly to Leicester.

He needn't have worried; he's thrived under Ranieri and played 34 games.

Deemed surplus to requirements in Germany he was, nevertheless, a key stabilizing influence in a Leicester team with minimal European experience. Playing at left back, he's a set piece specialist and easily fitted into Ranieri's strategy of moving the ball quickly up the field for Vardy to chase down.

He scored for Schalke against Real Madrid in 2015 so will bring some much-needed know-how once the Champions League campaign gets under way.

DANNY SIMPSON

A product of Manchester United's youth academy, Simpson was sent out on loan to Belgian club Royal Antwerp, Sunderland, Ipswich, Blackburn and Newcastle United before leaving for the Magpies in January 2010.

After 100 appearances in the North-East, the full back joined Harry Rednapp's QPR on a free and actually played against Leicester during their Championship winning season.

But like Jamie Vardy, he's had his fair share of trouble in the past. Indeed, only a last minute court action enabled him to join his teammates on their end-of-season celebrations.

85

In June 2015 - before the start of the "Miracle Season" - he was convicted of assaulting his ex-girlfriend Stephanie Ward, the mother of his child, at their home in Worsley, Manchester the previous December.

A court heard that police arrived to find Simpson straddling Ward, his partner of eight years, with both hands around her throat. The footballer, who previously dated X-Factor judge Tulisa Contostavlos, was led away in handcuffs, leaving Ward "crying hysterically and cowering" in the corner of the living room.

According to the Daily Telegraph, PC Gareth Hughes, the first policeman on the scene, said: "I could hear screams, crying, then silence. I could then hear choking. I could see a small female lying in a prone position facing up. She was about three metres away from me.

"I saw a male who I now know to be Daniel Simpson straddling across her with his hands firmly placed round her neck. He was sitting on her on his knees. I initially heard choking when I entered the room. He seemed startled by my sudden presence. I had to drag him by his arm."

In spite of the circumstances of the arrest, Simpson initially denied all the charges but he was eventually found guilty and sentenced to 300 hours of community service.

With only half the hours completed, he complained that media intrusion made the work untenable and was allowed to swap for a 21-day curfew, meaning he had to be home every night during that period, similar to Vardy's punishment for assault as a younger man.

When he went back before the court saying the curfew would spoil his title jollies and a planned club trip to Thailand, the judge refused to allow him to escape with a fine, saying that would make little difference to a sportsman earning £35,000-a-week.

Appealing the decision, he was finally freed from the curfew on the understanding he would complete his community work later in the summer.

While Simpson may have been an integral part of the Leicester dream team, the entire episode left many women - and male - fans with a sour taste in their mouths.

WES MORGAN

Leicester City's skipper and the heart of Leicester's mighty defence, Morgan has spent almost his entire career as a Championship player. He played over 400 times for Nottingham Forest before switching to their East Midlands rivals.

Nottingham born and schooled initially at Notts County before joining Forest at the age of 15, Morgan was in the Reds' first team setup for eight-and-a-half years before joining the blues in January 2012. He is also a Jamaican international.

His only other club was non-league Kidderminster. Morgan's leadership has never really been in doubt, but his strength and ability to nullify Premier League attackers has been a revelation, as were the crucial goals he scored during the stretch.

He's the co-owner of Blue Ink, a Leicester tattoo studio.

ROBERT HUTH

The big 6'3" German centre back must have thought his better days were over when he signed for Leicester in the summer of 2015.

Beginning his career with Chelsea, he made his debut at 17 under then manager Claudio Ranieri, and won two Premier League medals during Jose

Mourinho's first spell at Stamford Bridge despite a constant battle for a place behind the likes of John Terry and Ricardo Carvalho.

He has 19 caps for his country and played for Germany in the 2006 World Cup in his homeland. Moves to Middlesborough in 2006 and then on to Stoke City three years later established him as a solid, if not spectacular, presence in the division.

Like Morgan, he scored key goals for the club. One of the three won his side a vital win against closest rivals Tottenham.

DANNY DRINKWATER

Another Manchester United Academy reject, Drinkwater came into his own pulling the strings in Leicester's central midfield.

He's openly admitted that any dreams he may have had of winning the Premier League faded four years earlier when he was let go by United.

Drinkwater's another player who put his time in navigating the lower divisions during loan appearances with Cardiff City, Watford and Barnsley. He also made 37 appearances in League 1 while on loan with Huddersfield Town during the 2009/10 season.

With his passing accuracy, Drinkwater was given a vital role in Leicester's winning strategy - collect the ball in midfield and look to pass it ahead of the opponent's defenders for Vardy to chase. His efficiency at doing just that - while controlling the pace of his team's play - earned him an England call-up.

N'GOLO KANTE

Arguably the discovery of the season. A tenacious tackler and skilful ball handler, Kante alternatively broke up attacks and launched his own team's forward drives, all while getting just three yellow cards all season. The secret? His immaculate timing.

Kante was Ranieri's first signing in August 2015 and the most important addition to the squad. Yet before his arrival in England, he had been toiling in the lower leagues of France's less-than-competitive system.

Born in Paris in 1991, Kanté's footballing career began with US Boulogne, where he came through the youth ranks to make his first team debut against AS Monaco in May 2012. His impressive performances for US Boulogne saw Caen swoop for his talents in 2013. That faith was quickly rewarded as Kante played 38 games en route to a promotion from the French Ligue 2 in the 2013/14 campaign.

A further 37 appearances and two goals in 2014/15 underlined his potential, but the credit goes to Leicester's scouting team for getting in first for a player who is now an international and being chased by Paris St-Germain and a host of other big clubs.

RIYAD MAHREZ

The biggest problem for Leicester with the Premier League Player of the Year will be keeping hold of him. Real Madrid has already been in contact with the player's representatives and he's also being linked with Barcelona, Manchester United, Arsenal and Liverpool.

Before the season started, none of them gave him a second look.

His ability to glide past defenders and his goalscoring prowess changed all that - suddenly his slender build wasn't such a problem. Like Kante he came from the French Ligue 2, where he starred with lowly Club Le Havre.

89

The French-born Algerian international made 20 appearances for Le Havre in 2013/14, scoring six times and providing five assists from the right side of midfield, before joining the Foxes in January 2014.

Scout Steve Walsh was actually monitoring Mahrez's teammate Ryan Mendes when he spotted the Algerian, who'd never even heard of Leicester and thought they were a rugby team.

Mahrez was one of four Leicester players named in the PFA Team of the Year in April 2016, and later that month he won the PFA Players' Player of the Year award for his 17 goals and 11 assists. He was the first African to earn the accolade.

When Leicester finished the season as champions, Mahrez became the first Algerian to win a Premier League medal.

MARC ALBRIGHTON

After 16 years with Aston Villa, Albrighton moved to Leicester in the summer of 2104 and ended up celebrating with a league title medal the same year his boyhood club was relegated to the Championship.

The signs were already on the wall at Villa when the winger was shipped down a division to Wigan on loan during the 2013-14 season, but he's enjoyed a renaissance at his new club with six key assists.

"It was a real shock when Villa let me go," said Albrighton about his exit in the summer of 2014.

"I was led to believe I was getting a contract, and then I found out two days after the season finished that I wasn't.

"That's football," he told the Express. "Decisions are made day in, day out at clubs – and I was just another decision. But it was definitely a shock. It did hurt, obviously. You want to play for your boyhood club from when you are a kid all the way through and be a Steven Gerrard-type player with just one club in the Premier League.

"That's your dream when you are growing up. But the reality is it doesn't happen very often nowadays."

Gerrard never managed a Premier League title during his stellar career. A few clubs moved for Albrighton but he said: "Leicester was the one that stood out. I know there was a risk, because they were a promoted club, of not making the grade and going back to the Championship.

"I was willing to take that chance. I could see the team spirit, the togetherness in the squad. It was fantastic and something I wanted to be part of."

SHINJI OKAZAKI

He may be the Bundesliga's all-time leading Japanese scorer, but Okazaki was unknown in British football before joining Leicester in June 2015.

Of course, he will say that nobody in Japan had heard of Leicester City either.

At club level things began for Okazaki back in Japan with J-League side Shimizu S-Pulse, with whom he signed his first professional contract in 2005. After making his debut at the age of 19 he went on to score 49 goals in 154 games for the Club before moving to Bundesliga side VfB Stuttgart in January 2011.

After a move to Mainz in 2013 he scored 15 goals to help the team to a seventh placed finish and Europa League qualification.

91

The "Samurai striker" isn't so much a fan of Ranieri's pizza, however. He prefers fish and chips.

LEONARDO ULLOA

The big Argentinian came to Leicester after spending 18 months with Championship side Brighton and Hove Albion. Nothing wrong with that, but it was still a big step up to fire some of the key goals that helped his new team.

Gus Poyet, his manager at Brighton, had no doubts that Ulloa would rise to the occasion when his big chance came after Vardy was banned for two matches as a result of his "dive" against West Ham.

Ulloa kept his cool to hammer home a game-saving penalty after Vardy's dismissal and then proved an able replacement for his colleague.

"His penalty against the Hammers showed me two things," said Poyet. "One because I know him as a person and a player that likes to assume responsibility. And two - as they say in Spain he as a couple of cojones. Big ones."

ANDY KING

The playing staff's most loyal servant, he joined Leicester's academy in 2004 and played in the League 1, Championship and Premier League winning sides.

The highest scoring midfielder in the club's history, he fittingly grabbed a goal in the final home game of the season in the 3-1 thrashing of Everton.

King was in the team the night a 3-2 defeat at Brighton in October 2008 dropped them to sixth in League One, Leicester's lowest ever league position.

And he played in the 3-0 win at Newcastle last November when Leicester moved to the top of the Premier League for the first time since the opening days of the season.

He has worked for seven managers at Leicester - including Nigel Pearson twice - and made almost 300 league appearances. It certainly hasn't all been roses. He was a ball boy at Stamford Bridge and dreamed of a pro career with Chelsea, where he was on the books as a boy.

Chelsea let him go when the manager was...Claudio Ranieri.

"It was the start of the (Roman) Abramovich era and they said it wasn't good enough to be the best lad in London or even England any more," he told the Daily Mail. "You had to be the best in Europe and they said they would be looking for someone else in my position. I took it on the chin. I could see it. They only kept three or four. I only have good memories from Chelsea but it's nice to go back as a Premier League champion to a club that kicked you out at 16.

"The manager is probably more keen to rub salt in the wounds than I am. The young players would be ball boys so I was always sitting near to Claudio or across the other side from him. I saw a lot of him. He used to be a lot more animated then. It is strange having watched him give out tactics and now it's turned full circle for him and for me."

JEFF SCHLUPP

Powerfully built Schlupp joined Leicester's academy at 11 and played at every youth level before breaking into the first team.

Like many of his teammates, he was a nearly man until this season. He spent a month on trial at Manchester United in March 2013 and almost secured a contract at Old Trafford, but returned unsigned to Leicester.

"I don't think I could ever turn down a move to Manchester United, but I didn't get the opportunity at the time. The trial I had moulded me into the player I am today," he told the Mirror.

"But Leicester City is my club, it has always been my club, and I'm very grateful to be here now.

"I was there for six weeks. It was supposed to be a week to start off, just to have a look at things, but it got extended and I found myself training with the first team and the Under-21s.

Then it got to the Champions League knock-out stages and I was just with the 21s.

"It was a great experience, of course, training with players of that calibre, and I'm forever grateful for getting the opportunity to see what it was like to be with a top team. It was the same summer when Sir Alex retired, and Mick Phelan and Rene Meulensteen also left, so nothing actually was said at the end of it and nothing came of it."

Sclupp became the first Foxes player in 66 years to score a hat-trick on his debut in a League Cup tie against Rotherham in August 2011. The German-born Ghanaian international was a key member of the back-up squad in the run to the title.

MARCIN WASILEWSKI

The burly Polish international joined the club in September 2013 on a one-year contract and has been there ever since.

His chief success before that was with Belgian side Anderlecht, where he lifted three league titles.

Back-up to Morgan and Huth, he represented Poland at the European Championship Finals in 2008 and 2012 and in October 2012, during the 2014 World Cup qualification campaign, captained his country in their 1-1 draw with England in Warsaw.

Who on earth would have predicted a Hollywood ending to Jamie Vardy's rollercoaster football career?

The player's extraordinary rise to the top is already being developed as a major film plot with big names fighting over the leading roles. But friends say Vardy and his wife Becky already have their eyes on a move across the Atlantic to follow in the footsteps of David and Victoria Beckham to settle with their family in Los Angeles.

With fame and success coming relatively late in Vardy's career, he is understood to be considering a move to the Los Angeles Galaxy or another top team in America's Major League Soccer within the next few years.

It would be a another huge upheaval for the former Sheffield factory worker but a Leicester insider said Vardy is looking to secure the best possible future for his family and Becky is excited about the possibilities of starting a new life in the California sunshine.

"Jamie and Becky have talked a lot about moving to Los Angeles one day and all of his success this season has really made anything possible," said the friend. "As I understand it the MLS has already been asking questions about Jamie and monitoring his interest.

"Becky and the kids will go out to California with Jamie at the end of July when he will be playing an exhibition match against Paris Saint-Germain at the StubHub Centre, where the LA Galaxy play their home games.

"It will be a fantastic opportunity for them to look at houses in the area and for Becky and the kids to decide if it's somewhere they'd like to live. It hasn't been easy for them at home these past few months because everyone ion the area now knows where they live. I'm sure he will ask David Beckham what he thinks the next time they meet when Jamie's playing for England."

For Vardy, who didn't dare dream of playing in the top flight just four years ago, playing abroad would be a chance to write another chapter in his amazing story.

"He would be incredible in the MLS, even if he waits a couple more years to play some more in the Premier League," said the source. "He keeps himself in great condition and he will still be running at defenders and harassing defences when he's 35. He hasn't come all this way for it to fizzle out."

In the meantime, Vardy's life story is being plotted out for a big budget film that's already generating Oscar talk.

There has yet to be a definitive soccer movie like *Rocky* or *Rudy, Remember The Titans* or *Field of Dreams*.

There's *Goal!*, of course, and *Goal 2*, but they don't really capture the heart of the world's favourite team sport. The Vardy story, however, has all the plot points a screenwriter could ever hope for.

There's the rags to riches struggle, the setbacks with the law, the beautiful girlfriend, the family strife and the happy ending.

And there's an entire back-up cast of teammates whose joint triumph is being widely heralded as the greatest story in the history of sport.

There's already enough there to convince Adran Butchart, the writer behind the *Goal!* films, that he might be on to something. He spent the final months of the season observing the euphoria around Leicester's race to the finish line, and even went so far as to get Vinny Jones, the former Wimbledon hardman-turned-movie tough guy, to portray Nigel Pearson in the movie about his striker protégé's life.

Butchart told Newsweek he decided to green-light the project the night Vardy beat the record for successive goals in games in the Premier League against Manchester United.

"I was aware of Jamie in the build-up to breaking the record and some of the background to the story," said Butchart, "and it seemed like he had what we want out of a movie. We decided to make the movie when he broke the record. That seemed to be the moment, and there was enough then to make a film with his story alone.

"People said why not make a movie about [Cristiano] Ronaldo or [Lionel] Messi or one of these other guys who are more famous. My response was always that it is less interesting to watch a movie about some guy that's picked up by a football academy at nine years old and spends a life eating skinless chicken breasts and going to bed at 9pm, compared to Jamie who has had an exciting, interesting, diverse, sometimes controversial, but fun life, which will light up the screen. That is what drew me to Jamie."

Vardy, who is also writing 'My Story,' a memoir charting his long journey, has been cooperating with Butchart, along with Becky and his agent, John Morris.

"It's been really important, and I've got enough experience from football films to know that whatever I do can't interrupt the real business of what they're doing, which is winning football matches. I've been very, very careful to stay out and not risk affecting things on the field," Butchart told Newsweek.

Twilight actor Robert Pattinson, *One Direction* star Louis Tomlinson, and Hollywood heartthrob Zac Efron are among the names linked to the Vardy role. One actor who really fancied the part, Scottish actor James McAvoy, was disappointed, however.

McAvoy, an avid Celtic fan, told Britain's Daily Express newspaper: "It is my time, this is my time! Play a guy playing football? I would love that! Vardy's party - bringing it to Hollywood!"

The X-Men star, who recently split from his wife of nine years Anne-Marie Duff, even joked the sporting role would bag him an Oscar, adding, "I'm a shoo-in. I'm a shoo-in for next year's Oscars I know it!"

But Butchart dashed the actor's hopes, saying he thinks McAvoy, 37, is a too old.

"We are delighted to hear James is a Vardy fan and wants to be in the movie," Butchart said, "Sadly, he's a little too old to play Jamie but there are other roles that would be perfect for him and he'd still get to kick a football!"

Manchester United legend Eric Cantona has been mentioned as a possible Ranieri on the big screen and Game of Thrones actress Emilia Clarke is being lined up as Becky.

"The response was incredible," said Butchart. "People are getting in touch everyday from all aspects of entertainment asking how they can be involved. Financiers offering to put up the money, distributors, actors, countless candidates to play Jamie Vardy, and a bunch of the other roles. There are people we like and we have had conversations with people."

He said Vinnie Jones is already lined up. "That came about because the Leicester Mercury ran a poll of who people wanted to see as playing Nigel Pearson. The choices were Vinnie, Jason Statham or Ray Stevenson. And 74 percent of them voted for Vinnie. So, we got in touch with him and said, 'This has happened, what do you think?' He wrote back and said, 'Cool, I'm in.'

"I think we would all love to see him [in the film]. This film belongs to the people of Leicester as much as anyone, so I would love to make their wishes come true."

He said the fact-based film - projected to start shooting in October 2016 and be released the following summer, will be very different to his previous chronicling of a fictional Mexican immigrant who goes on to play first for Newcastle and then Real Madrid. "There are definitely similarities and I think that, for me, it's a logical next step in the project because I have a track record of doing these movies," he said. "Tonally, this film will be different because we have a very different central character. He has a different temperament from the kid who was in the *Goal!* films.

"One of the other huge differences is that *Goal!* is fictional characters in a fictional world that was based on reality."

Vardy and Becky are aware the memoir and film will turn their lives into an open book.

"It's totally throwing ourselves out there and there will be no skeletons left in the closet by the end of it," said Becky.

"The film is probably the most surreal element of all of this," she told the Mirror. "It's incredible that somebody wants to document Jamie's life. Even six months ago you would never have dreamt it was possible but we've been in talks with Adrian for a while now.

"We're piecing together Jamie's life and then our life together as a couple. Everything will have to be dealt with but we're prepared for that."

Despite their dreams of a move to California, Becky insists that she and Vardy are nothing like the Beckhams, aka Posh and Becks. She says they're more than happy with their low key homebody lives away from the stadium lights.

But if the movie proves as successful as her husband's slow-burning career, Vards and Becks may eclipse even the Beckhams.

The striker doesn't plan to change any time soon on the field. He will do what he does best - scoring goals - and keep believing that everything else will take care of itself.

There's one thing you can be certain of - Jamie Vardy's Having a Party...and it's far from over.

Jamie Vardy may do most of his talking with his feet, but he still likes to say it as it is.

Here are 50 quotes from Vardy on Vardy.

1. *I remember at school we went to an army camp for a day. We did the official army bleep test and I got to level 14.5. I think the closest person to me that day got to level 10. Fitness has always been one of my strengths. I can do all the long-distance runs. When I was at school and we entered the competitions I used to do the 100m, 200m and the 1500m as well, so it's never just been a pace thing.*

2. *When you get into an academy and you are playing football every day of the week that is all you ever want to do.*

3. *When I got released for being too small it was a real heartache. That was one of the reasons I stopped because I thought I would never be a profes-sional.*

4. *When I got released by Wednesday I literally stopped playing for a while. It was the lowest point in my career. It was hard to take.*

5. *I was out one night with a friend who wore a hearing aid. Two lads, for no reason, thought it would be funny to start knocking him and attacking him. I am not proud of what I did but I stuck up for him and defended him, as I would for any mate. It ended up getting me into a bit of trouble.*

6. (On wearing an electronic tag after being convicted of assault). *I couldn't go out, I was locked in the house. All my mates would be out but I was sat at home. Luckily, I had a big DVD collection so I would watch loads of movies every night. It was something I had to learn from and I did.*

7. *That is one of the things that has made me the person sat in front of you. It was hard. It had an effect on my family as well because I am in the house constantly. It was tough not being able to do what any normal 20-year-old wants to do.*

8. *I was still able to play football but on a few occasions I had to leap over fences and get in the car to get back to avoid breaking my curfew. My mum and dad would pick me up. The away games, if they were too far, I could only play an hour. I would have to come off, hope we were winning and jump straight back into the car to get home in time.*

9. *You could actually wear the bracelet as an ankle guard. It would protect your ankles. There was no way of breaking it. You could hit it with a hammer and it wouldn't come off. It was unbreakable.*

10. *I got a move to Halifax, which was brilliant, but the work was taking its toll on me. It was doing my back in so I decided to just quit and live off the football money. Luckily, three days later, I signed for Fleetwood.*

11. *I went to college and a friend got me playing for his Sunday side, I wanted to get back into it. After that, I ended up playing for Stockbridge Park Steels as a youth player, then I had broke into the reserves and then the first team.*

12. *I was working full-time at the time so it was tough. There were long hours at work in the day and then playing football at night.*

13. *We had to do a lot of heavy lifting into ovens and the shelves we had to put items on were way above my height. When you have to do that on a daily basis and you are lifting about 100 times a day it damages your back so it was time to stop. It didn't stop me playing football. If anything, I was playing football the night before and then ringing up work the next day and saying I was injured to get off work, to be honest.*

14. *I remember my first wage with Stocksbridge. I was a youth player and just to get called up to the first team it was 30 pound a week. I had never earned money through football before. I was happy to get that. We used to get 200 or 300 fans watching, unless we played one of the big local clubs like Wednesday or Sheffield United.*

15. *Those were the experience that made me the person I am today.*

16. (On The Day England Manager Roy Hodgson Came To Watch): *We were live on television but I think it was a bad game for him to come to. It was*

very windy and the pitch was like sand dunes. There were bobbles everywhere but we won the game.

17. *I had to do it* (streak naked) *once as a forfeit at Fleetwood. I can't remember why, but it was normally something to do with being late or the worst prank of the day.*

18. *Chat sh*t, get banged.*

19. *I was just concentrating on helping Leicester pull away from that relegation zone.*

20. *My life has changed, but I'm not money-motivated at all; that's the last thing on my mind. I just want to play football and that's how I've always been. To be honest with you, that shows in my performances, that I'm in a happy place, knowing that I'm doing the job that I love.*

21. *There has been a lot of focus on me, I think, obviously, if I let it affect me performance, I have kept my head down and not tried to let it sink in my head and just concentrate, it's just another game where we wanted to get 3 points in.*

22. *I never thought I could make it to the Premier League. I just wanted to keep improving as much as I could and see where that got me.*

23. *The best present I've ever given someone is myself.*

24. *When I am on the pitch I have to lead from the front and be aggressive because of my size. It lead to my nickname* (The Cannon!)

25. *It really has been a dream come true.*

26. *If I'm played out of position I'll always give 100%, but everyone knows I would rather play down the middle. I also think for myself, and the club as a whole, the year's experience last season has done us the world of good. The confidence in knowing that we can give teams a game, which showed in the run-in when we pulled away from the relegation zone, helped us all out and we've just carried that on.*

27. *There's still a long way to go, I'll get back on the training field and look at how I can break Watford's defense but I need my teammates as well.*

28. *That's how every striker should feel otherwise there's no point in being a striker, it's as simple as that, that's what I get paid for – to put the ball in the back of the net.*

29. *Everything I'm touching is going in. Long may that continue.*

30. (On Becky) *She's changed me. She's such a calming influence. When I was living on my own, for a footballer it's easy to do the things that you're not supposed to, or not what the sport science team says. For example, if there's a packet of crisps, you're going to eat them. The same with a packet of sweets.*

Go to bed at a certain time? You're not going to if you're on your own. Having Becky and the kids there is brilliant for me.

31. *Anyone know any decent bed places in Leicester.*

32. *There was a lot of hard work that has gone into this, I have to still pinch myself most days before I even got here. I have been given a chance now and hopefully I will get to show it on the big stage. You would never thought, where I have come from, this was ever on the cards.*

33. *I've not thought about record at all. If someone else gets the goal that gets us three points I'll be happy.*

34. *No pressure, one game, one goal!*

35. *I did not really expect it, but I did not set myself any targets either. I just wanted to make sure I improved on last year, and I've managed to do that. To get the 10 in a row is brilliant, but the main thing is the points for Leicester.*

36. *I pinch myself every day anyway. Everyone knows the road I have had in the game, and how I have managed to get myself to where I am today. Obviously it has been tough, but it is nice to be among those names.*

37. *It would be unbelievable [to break the record], but I would only want to get another if we got the three points.*

38. *With Ruud van Nistelrooy holding the record before, you can't get much better than that – it was a brilliant message from him.*

39. (On What He Said After Scoring in 11th Consecutive match) *Because the Man United fans were singing Ruud van Nistelrooy, I said: 'Me, me, all effing me' ... Live on Sky. Again. I need to calm down a bit. I was just lost in the moment, that's what it was. And, to be fair, I saw the replay of the goal and you can actually see a couple of Man U fans clapping.*

40. (On the Streak) *This is the top-flight all-time record and it's set by a Sheffield United player, so being a Sheffield Wednesday fan I'd love to beat it.*

41. (On the attraction of playing in the Champions League) *You'd have to say the likes of Messi and Ronaldo. They're obviously the world's best and they have been for years, but we still know there's a long way to go until that might happen and we know that we've got to take each game as they come.*

42. (On Not Making BBC's Sports Personality Of The Year) *That's fine by me, I hate wearing a suit.*

43. (On the Euros) *Obviously I want to make sure that I'm involved in the squad and I know that's down to myself. But I think you see with the players that are involved there, they're all class and they're a close knit group as well and to be honest with you we can go far and we know that.*

44. *Wowzers. What's happening in life? But if that's what they want to do, then so be it.*

45. *Each one will give 100%. We put our bodies on the line for each other.*

46. *If you had asked me back then I would never have thought I would have signed for Leicester City.*

47. *I was just at Fleetwood and we were on a mission to get into the Football League. I thought that was where I would be after we got promoted as well. I never thought this (his England call-up) would happen either.*

48. *My phone was just vibrating in my pocket constantly. I left it all until Sunday morning and then worked my way through everything, which is not easy when you've got Twitter, WhatsApp, text messages, Instagram, etc. But some of the messages were unbelievable.*

50. *Confidence is sky high, but we're also all very grounded. We know in football nothing can be taken for granted. That's why every week as soon as we finish the game, if we've got the three points we are straight away focusing on the next game and the training that goes into it.*

Any worries that the off season upheaval at the club would lead to another relegation struggle were quickly dispelled in the opening game against Sunderland when Leicester scored three times in the first half an hour, with both Jamie Vardy and Riyad Mahrez getting in on the act in a pattern that was to last all season long.

When Vardy was misfiring, Mahrez would take over and vice versa. After a win against Slaven Bilic's resurgent West Ham United and resolute performances against Spurs and Bournemouth, people were starting to sit up and take notice, even if nobody really believed it was much more than a flash in the pan.

The home win against Aston Villa in mid-September suggested there may be more to this Leicester City season than anyone could have guessed. After twice falling behind, they scored twice in the final 10 minutes to steal the victory.

The first win set a tone, as the Foxes remained unbeaten in all competitions until a humbling 2-5 home defeat to Arsenal in late September. If anything, the loss inspired the team to strive even harder and they went on a run, taking 26 points from the next 10 games to top the table at Christmas 2015. This was "Vardy time" with the No. 9 netting in 11 games in a row to break the Premier League record.

The pundits - who never really believed until right near the end - pointed to the 6 points Leicester took from the next 5 games as proof that they couldn't maintain their unlikely title challenge. But Robert Huth's late winner at Spurs would turn out to be immensely important in the final run-in.

Meanwhile, a stunning Vardy volley from outside the box to help his team to a 2-0 win against Liverpool helped rebuild momentum, and a 3-1 victory against Manchester City underlined the team's title credentials and took them 5 points clear at the top.

Still Ranieri kept smiling, kept underplaying expectations. Sure this was fun, he would say, but there's such a long way still to go.

Beaten in the dying seconds by Arsenal at the Emirates could have left Leicester's resolve crumbling. Instead, it had a galvanising effect, and the team didn't lose again all season.
Kaspar Schmeichel kept six clean sheets in the next seven games and even Vardy's sending off for a dive against West Ham leading to a two-match suspension couldn't stop their winning momentum.

With just a few games left to play, only Tottenham could catch them. When the flying Spurs team was stopped in its tracks by a Chelsea side playing for pride after a disastrous title defence, the Premier League was won with two games to spare.

As the 2015-16 season drew to a close, Leicester City raised the Premier League trophy, Mahrez won PFA Player of the Year, Vardy took the FWA prize, Kante got the player's award and Ranieri was Manager of the Year.

Not one of those names would have been on anyone's list at the outset of the campaign.

Ultimately though, Leicester City's season wasn't about individuals; it was a team triumph, quite possibly the most astounding in English football history.

SEASON STATS

~ Leicester won the title with just 44.8 per cent of possession - only West Brom and Sunderland saw less of the ball.

~ Leicester scored in all but three of their Premier League matches, whereas title rivals Arsenal and Tottenham each failed to score on four occasions in home games alone.

~ Only four Premier League champions have won the title by a greater margin of points than Leicester (10) - Manchester United in 1999/2000 (18), Chelsea 2004/05 (12), Arsenal 2003/04 and Manchester United 2012/13 (11).

~ Wes Morgan became the third outfield player in Premier League history to play every minute of a title-winning season (after Gary Pallister in 1992/93 and John Terry in 2014/15).

GAME-BY-GAME

Saturday 7 May 2016

17:30   Leicester 3 - 1   Everton   King Power Stadium

Sunday 1 May 2016

14:05   Man Utd 1 - 1   Leicester Old Trafford

Sunday 24 April 2016

16:15   Leicester 4 - 0   Swansea King Power Stadium

112

Sunday 17 April 2016

13:30   Leicester 2 - 2   West Ham   King Power Stadium

Sunday 10 April 2016

13:30   Sunderland   0 - 2   Leicester Stadium of Light

Sunday 3 April 2016

13:30   Leicester 1 - 0   Southampton   King Power Stadium

Saturday 19 March 2016

15:00   Crystal Palace   0 - 1   Leicester Selhurst Park

Monday 14 March 2016

20:00   Leicester 1 - 0   Newcastle   King Power Stadium

Saturday 5 March 2016

17:30   Watford   0 - 1   Leicester Vicarage Road

Tuesday 1 March 2016

19:45   Leicester 2 - 2   West Brom   King Power Stadium

Saturday 27 February 2016

15:00   Leicester 1 - 0   Norwich   King Power Stadium

Sunday 14 February 2016

113

12:00   Arsenal   2 - 1   Leicester Emirates Stadium

Saturday 6 February 2016

12:45   Man City 1 - 3   Leicester Etihad Stadium

Tuesday 2 February 2016

19:45   Leicester 2 - 0   Liverpool King Power Stadium

Saturday 23 January 2016

15:00   Leicester 3 - 0   Stoke   King Power Stadium

Saturday 16 January 2016

17:30   Aston Villa   1 - 1   Leicester Villa Park

Wednesday 13 January 2016

20:00   Spurs   0 - 1   Leicester White Hart Lane

Saturday 2 January 2016

15:00   Leicester 0 - 0   Bournemouth   King Power Stadium

Tuesday 29 December 2015

19:45   Leicester 0 - 0   Man City King Power Stadium

Saturday 26 December 2015

15:00   Liverpool 1 - 0   Leicester Anfield

Saturday 19 December 2015

15:00   Everton   2 - 3   Leicester Goodison Park

Monday 14 December 2015

20:00   Leicester 2 - 1   Chelsea   King Power Stadium

Saturday 5 December 2015

15:00   Swansea 0 - 3   Leicester Liberty Stadium

Saturday 28 November 2015

17:30   Leicester 1 - 1   Man Utd King Power Stadium

Saturday 21 November 2015

15:00   Newcastle   0 - 3   Leicester St. James' Park

Saturday 7 November 2015

15:00   Leicester 2 - 1   Watford   King Power Stadium

Saturday 31 October 2015

15:00   West Brom   2 - 3   Leicester The Hawthorns

Saturday 24 October 2015

15:00   Leicester 1 - 0   Crystal Palace   King Power Stadium

Saturday 17 October 2015

15:00   Southampton   2 - 2   Leicester St. Mary's Stadium

Saturday 3 October 2015

15:00   Norwich 1 - 2   Leicester Carrow Road

Saturday 26 September 2015

15:00   Leicester 2 - 5   Arsenal King Power Stadium

Saturday 19 September 2015

15:00   Stoke   2 - 2   Leicester Britannia Stadium

Sunday 13 September 2015

16:00   Leicester 3 - 2   Aston Villa   King Power Stadium

Saturday 29 August 2015

15:00   Bournemouth   1 - 1   Leicester Vitality Stadium

Saturday 22 August 2015

15:00   Leicester 1 - 1   Spurs   King Power Stadium

Saturday 15 August 2015

15:00   West Ham   1 - 2   Leicester Boleyn Ground

Saturday 8 August 2015

15:00   Leicester 4 - 2   Sunderland   King Power Stadium

FINAL PREMIER LEAGUE STANDINGS 2015-16 SEASON

1. Leicester City

2. Arsenal

3. Tottenham Hotspur

4. Manchester City

5. Manchester United

6. Southampton

7. West Ham United

8. Liverpool

9. Stoke City

10. Chelsea

11. Everton

12. Swansea City

13. Watford

14. West Bromwich Albion

15. Crystal Palace

16. AFC Bournemouth

17.Sunderland

18. Newcastle United

19. Norwich City

20. Aston Villa

~THE END~

Printed in Great Britain
by Amazon